Financial Calculations
Practical Guide with Python and R

Engin Demirel, Ph.D.

Table of Contents

Financial Calculations Practical Guide with Python and R

All Rights Reserved

Copyright © 2023 Engin Demirel, Ph.D.

Introduction

This book provides readers with a thorough road map for understanding critical ideas by covering various financial computations. The book is divided into nine sections covering essential subjects such as portfolio optimization, risk management, and time value of money. In these parts, readers will find a carefully chosen to set of average twenty calculations per subject for more than two hundred examples with the financial calculations. This guide's strength is its practical approach, which provides theoretical understanding and valuable solutions utilizing the Python and R programming languages.

The book also explains each computation methodically, simply expressing the underlying financial concepts. Formulas are provided in an easily understood format to guarantee that the theory is well understood. The real value of this book is providing readers with ready-to-use R and Python lines of code, making the theory-to-practice transfer effortlessly.

Financial Calculations Practical Guide with Python and R book is an essential resource book for anybody interested in bridging the knowledge gap between academia and business, whether a student or a financial professional looking to expand their analytical toolset. With the help of this carefully designed book, readers can unlock the complexity of financial calculations and equip themselves with the knowledge and abilities needed to negotiate the complexities of finance confidently and accurately.

In the book, each chapter begins with the definition and specification of the necessary functions for financial calculations. Subsequently, the code lines required for R are provided first, followed immediately by those necessary for Python (these sections are highlighted in gray). These codes allow you to experiment with and make the necessary adjustments. The nature and usage of the code are then explained. Following this, an exemplary dataset for financial calculations is presented. The solutions for both R and Python programming languages are demonstrated using this sample data, with the R solution showcased first and followed by the Python solution. Finally, for comparative analysis, the outputs of the solutions are separately displayed for both programming languages. This approach facilitates the utilization of practical coding examples in reader endeavors in both programming languages.

Simultaneously, readers can compare the differences in programming languages in the sample calculations. While the examples and demonstrations are intended for practical usage, detailed studies, code packages, and educational materials for coding in both languages can be accessed through the links provided at the end of the book. There is no specific sequence of topics outside the book's chapter headings. Readers can locate and try any example from the table of contents.

Also, one of the book's fundamental objectives is to create a practical guide that combines financial education with coding languages.

Engin Demirel, Ph.D

How to use and install Python and R

R console installation

R is a popular software environment and programming language for financial and statistical computation. Your experience with financial data analysis and programming may be much improved by learning how to navigate its primary menu and using it effectively. The primary menu items and their functions in "R" are explained in detail below:

To install R, follow these steps:
Download R from this link
Choose the version compatible with your operating system.
Once the download is complete, open the installer.
Follow the installation wizard's instructions.
After the installation, open R to start using it.

Optionally, you can also install RStudio, an integrated development environment (IDE) for R, from this link
Launch RStudio and configure it to suit your preferences.

File Menu: The File menu allows you to create new scripts, open existing files, and manage your R project's directory. You can also save, export, and import data files for analysis.
Edit Menu: This menu provides essential editing functionalities, including copy, paste, find, and replace, and other text manipulation tools to streamline your coding process.
View Menu: You can customize the layout of your R environment using the View menu. It enables you to adjust the appearance of your workspace, manage script and console layouts, and control the visibility of various panels and tool windows.
Packages Menu: The Packages menu allows you to manage R packages efficiently. You can install, update, and remove packages, as well as load and unload them to access a wide range of additional functionalities and tools.
Plots Menu: This menu is dedicated to creating and customizing visualizations in R. You can generate various types of plots, adjust plot properties, and export plots for presentations and reports.
Tools Menu: The Tools menu provides access to additional utilities and functionalities that can enhance your R programming experience. It may

include features such as the R workspace, script editor, and global options, allowing you to customize your R environment to suit your specific requirements.

Session Menu: This menu enables you to manage your R session effectively. You can control the R interpreter, manage working directories, and access options to save or clear the current workspace.

Help Menu: The Help menu is a valuable resource that provides access to R documentation, manuals, and online resources. You can find information on functions, packages, and general R programming concepts to guide you through your coding and analysis tasks.

Copy and paste the selected calculation code, which is highlighted in gray in the book, to the "R console" screen and "enter" to execute the example. To delete screen on R console shortcuts are "cmd+alt+L" for mac and "Ctrl+L" for windows. This book serves as a practice guide. You may easily adapt the numerical examples to your own data.

Python usage

PyCharm is a powerful integrated development environment (IDE) for Python that offers a comprehensive set of tools and features to streamline the process of coding and developing Python applications. This is a text editor for Python which reader can use different options (such as: IDLE, Jupiter Notebooks, VSCode, Spyder, Sublime text, Command Line text editor).

To install PyCharm for Python, follow these steps:
Download PyCharm from this link
Choose the version compatible with your operating system.
Once the download is complete, open the installer.
Follow the installation wizard's instructions.
After the installation, launch PyCharm.
Configure PyCharm according to your preferences and settings.
On the welcome screen, click on "Create New Project."
Specify the location where you want to create the new project.
Click on your "Project name" at search projects screen or "open" button right upper corner.

The main menu of PyCharm is composed of several components arranged in an easy-to-use layout. Let's examine the main elements and features:

File Menu: The File menu allows you to create new projects, open existing ones, import files, and manage project settings.

Edit Menu: This menu is dedicated to editing features, including copy, paste, find, and replace, and other text manipulation tools.

View Menu: Here, you can customize the layout of your workspace, manage tool windows, and toggle various UI elements according to your preferences.

Navigate Menu: This menu is instrumental in navigating through your project, providing quick access to classes, files, symbols, and specific lines of code. It helps you efficiently move around your codebase.

Code Menu: The Code menu contains an excess of options for code analysis, formatting, and generation. You can find tools for refactoring, code inspections, and managing code style settings to ensure your code is clean and follows best practices.

Run Menu: This menu is essential for running and debugging your Python code. You can execute scripts, manage configurations, and analyze runtime behaviors to identify and fix any issues.

Tools Menu: Here, you can access various tools integrated into PyCharm, such as the built-in terminal, version control systems, and database management tools, facilitating a seamless development experience.

VCS Menu: This menu is dedicated to version control systems like Git. You can perform Git operations, manage branches, commit changes, and resolve merge conflicts directly from PyCharm.

Window Menu: This menu allows you to manage open windows, editor tabs, and tool windows within the PyCharm interface, enabling you to work on multiple files or projects simultaneously.

Copy and paste the selected calculation code, which is highlighted in gray in the book, to the "main.py" screen and click on "Run Main" or "^R" to execute the example. This book is a practice guide purpose. Feel free to change the numeric examples to your data.

How to install necessary packages in Pycharm:
Go to "File" > "Settings" > "Project: your_project_name" > "Python Interpreter."
Click on the '+' icon to add a new package.
Search for the package you want and click "Install Package."

These are the required packages for this book calculation examples:

"FinancialMaths, Pillow, appdirs, certifi charset-normalizer, contourpy, cycler, fonttools, frozendict html5lib, idna, importlib-resources, kiwisolver, Ixml, matplotlib, multitasking, numpy, numpy-financial, packaging, pandas, peewee, pip, pyparsing, python-dateutil, pytz, requests, scipy, setuptools, soupsieve ta tzdata, urllibe, webencodings, wheel, yfinance, zipp".

CHAPTER 1

This chapter consist best-known 20 finance formulas along with their corresponding code examples in both R and Python:

1. Compound Interest

Compound interest is the interest that is computed on the original principle of a loan or deposit, as well as the total interest that has accrued over time. Compound interest permits the investment or debt to expand over time, in contrast to simple interest, which simply calculates interest on the initial principal amount. Compound interest is characterized by the addition of interest to the principle as time goes on. This means that future interest computations are based on the greater principal amount. The amount owing on a loan, or the value of an investment increases exponentially because of this compounding effect.

Formula: $A = P * (1 + r/n)^{(nt)}$
Where:
- A = Final amount
- P = Principal amount
- r = Annual interest rate
- n = Number of times interest is compounded per year
- t = Number of years

```r
# R
compound_interest <- function(P, r, n, t) {
  A <- P * (1 + r/n)^(n*t)
  return(A)
}
```

```python
# Python
def compound_interest(P, r, n, t):
    A = P * (1 + r/n)**(n*t)
    return A
```

This formula calculates the future value (A) of an initial investment (P) with compound interest, given the interest rate (r), the number of compounding periods per year (n), and the number of years (t).

Let's walk through a numeric example to illustrate how the code works. For this example, let's assume:

- Initial investment (P): $1000
- Annual interest rate (r): 0.05 (5%)
- Compounding periods per year (n): 12 (monthly compounding)
- Number of years (t): 3

Using the provided code, we can calculate the compound interest in both R and Python.

```r
#R
P <- 1000
r <- 0.05
n <- 12
t <- 3
compound_interest <- function(P, r, n, t) {
  A <- P * (1 + r/n)^(n*t)
  return(A)
}
result_r <- compound_interest(P, r, n, t)
print(result_r)
```

```python
#Python
P = 1000
r = 0.05
n = 12
t = 3
def compound_interest(P, r, n, t):
  A = P * (1 + r/n)(n*t)
  return A
result_python = compound_interest(P, r, n, t)
print(result_python)
```

In both cases, the output will be the future value (A) of the investment after 3 years with monthly compounding:

Output:
1161.472

The result represents the value of the investment after 3 years, accounting for the compounded interest. The difference between the initial investment and the future value is the interest earned through compounding. In this example, an initial investment of $1000 at an annual interest rate of 5%, compounded monthly, would grow to $ 1161.472 after 3 years.

2. Present Value

Present Value (PV) represents the current value of a sum of money or a series of cash flows, discounted at a specific rate to reflect their current worth. In other words, it is the current value of a future amount of money, considering the time value of money.

Formula: $PV = FV / (1 + r)^t$
Where:
- PV = Present value
- FV = Future value
- r = Discount rate
- t = Number of years

```
# R
present_value <- function(FV, r, t) {
  PV <- FV / (1 + r)^t
  return(PV)
}
```

```
# Python
def present_value(FV, r, t):
    PV = FV / (1 + r)**t
    return PV
```

The provided code is an implementation of the present value formula in both R and Python. This formula calculates the present value (PV) of a future amount (FV) given a discount rate (r) and the number of years (t) into the future.

Let's go through a numeric example to demonstrate how the code works. For this example, let's assume:

- Future amount (FV): $1500
- Discount rate (r): 0.08 (8%)

- Number of years (t): 5

Using the given code, we can calculate the present value in both R and Python.

```r
R
FV <- 1500
r <- 0.08
t <- 5

present_value <- function(FV, r, t) {
  PV <- FV / (1 + r)^t
  return(PV)
}

result_r <- present_value(FV, r, t)
print(result_r)
```

```python
Python
FV = 1500
r = 0.08
t = 5

def present_value(FV, r, t):
    PV = FV / (1 + r)**t
    return PV

result_python = present_value(FV, r, t)
print(result_python)
```

In both cases, the output will be the present value (PV) of the $1500 future amount discounted back to the present using an 8% annual discount rate after 5 years:

Output
1020.8747955506294
The result represents the present value of the future amount. It indicates the amount that needs to be invested today to have a value of $1500 after 5 years, considering an 8% annual discount rate. In this example, the present value of the $1500 future amount is approximately $1020.87. This

reflects the fact that the value of money decreases over time due to factors like inflation and the opportunity cost of not investing it elsewhere.

3. Net Present Value (NPV)

Net Present Value (NPV) is the present value of future cash inflows and outflows of a project or investment, considering the time value of money. It helps assess the profitability of an investment by determining the net value of all cash flows over time.

Formula: $NPV = \Sigma(CF\_t / (1 + r)^t)$
Where:
- CF_t = Cash flow at time t
- r = Discount rate
- t = Time period

```R
# R
npv <- function(cash_flows, r) {
  t <- 0:length(cash_flows) - 1
  npv_value <- sum(cash_flows / (1 + r)^t)
  return(npv_value)
}
```

```python
# Python
def npv(cash_flows, r):
    t = list(range(len(cash_flows)))
    npv_value = sum([cf / (1 + r)**t for t, cf in zip(t, cash_flows)])
    return npv_value
```

The provided code implements the Net Present Value (NPV) calculation in both R and Python. NPV is a financial metric used to evaluate the profitability of an investment or project by discounting the future cash flows back to the present using a specified discount rate (r). Positive NPV indicates a potentially profitable investment, while negative NPV suggests the investment may not be worthwhile. This time, let's work with the following cash flows:

Year 0: -$2000 (Initial investment)
Year 1: $500
Year 2: $700
Year 3: $900
Year 4: $1100

Let's assume a discount rate (r) of 0.08 (8%).

Using the given code, we can calculate the NPV in both R and Python.

```R
R
cash_flows <- c(-2000, 500, 700, 900, 1100)
r <- 0.08
npv <- function(cash_flows, r) {
  t <- 0:(length(cash_flows) - 1)
  npv_value <- sum(cash_flows / (1 + r)^t)
  return(npv_value)
}
result_r <- npv(cash_flows, r)
print(result_r)
```

```Python
Python
cash_flows = [-2000, 500, 700, 900, 1100]
r = 0.08
def npv(cash_flows, r):
    t = list(range(len(cash_flows)))
    npv_value = sum([cf / (1 + r)**t for t, cf in zip(t, cash_flows)])
    return npv_value
result_python = npv(cash_flows, r)
print(result_python)
```

In both cases, the output will be the NPV of the cash flows, considering a discount rate of 10%:

Output
$ 586.0819921684624

The calculated NPV is approximately $586.08. This positive NPV suggests that the investment could potentially generate a profit when considering the discount rate of 8% and the series of cash flows over the four-year period.

4. Internal Rate of Return (IRR)

The Internal Rate of Return (IRR) represents the discount rate at which the net present value (NPV) of the cash flows from the investment becomes zero. It is the rate of return that makes the present value of all cash inflows equal to the present value of all cash outflows.

Formula: $NPV = \Sigma(CF\_t / (1 + IRR)^t) = 0$
Where IRR is the rate that makes NPV zero.

```R
# R
cash_flows <- c(-100, 30, 35, 40, 45, 50)
irr_equation <- function(rate, cash_flows) {
  t <- 0:(length(cash_flows) - 1)
  npv_value <- sum(cash_flows / (1 + rate)^t)
  return(npv_value)
}
irr_rate <- uniroot(irr_equation, interval = c(0, 1), cash_flows = cash_flows)$root
print(irr_rate)
```

```python
# Python
import numpy as np
from scipy.optimize import root_scalar
cash_flows = [-100, 30, 35, 40, 45, 50]
def irr_equation(rate, cash_flows):
    return sum([cf / (1 + rate)**t for t, cf in enumerate(cash_flows)])
irr_rate = root_scalar(irr_equation, args=(cash_flows,), bracket=[0, 1])
print(irr_rate.root)
```

Let's work through the provided code example step by step in both R and Python and calculate the Internal Rate of Return (IRR) for the given cash flows.

```R
R
cash_flows <- c(-100, 30, 35, 40, 45, 50)
irr_equation <- function(rate, cash_flows) {
  t <- 0:(length(cash_flows) - 1)
  npv_value <- sum(cash_flows / (1 + rate)^t)
  return(npv_value)
}

irr_rate <- uniroot(irr_equation, interval = c(0, 1), cash_flows = cash_flows)$root
print(irr_rate)
```

Note for Python:
Install both the numpy and scipy libraries by running the following commands:
pip install numpy
pip install scipy

Python
```
import numpy as np
from scipy.optimize import root_scalar
cash_flows = [-100, 30, 35, 40, 45, 50]
def irr_equation(rate, cash_flows):
    return sum([cf / (1 + rate)**t for t, cf in enumerate(cash_flows)])
irr_rate = root_scalar(irr_equation, args=(cash_flows,), bracket=[0, 1])
print(irr_rate.root)
```

Both the R and Python versions of the code do the same thing: they calculate the IRR for a series of cash flows. The cash flows for this example are:

- Year 0: -$100
- Year 1: $30
- Year 2: $35
- Year 3: $40
- Year 4: $45
- Year 5: $50

The provided code uses the IRR equation to find the discount rate at which the net present value of the cash flows becomes zero. This is done by numerically solving the equation using the `uniroot` function in R and the `root_scalar` function in Python.

Output
R: 0.2575398
Python: 0.2575161362187582

This IRR value suggests that the series of cash flows has an internal rate of return of approximately 25.75%. This means that, given the timing and amounts of the cash flows, the investment could potentially yield a return equivalent to that rate.

5. Capital Asset Pricing Model (CAPM)

CAPM is used to estimate the required rate of return for an investment based on its risk characteristics. It establishes a relationship between the expected return on an investment and its systematic risk. CAPM assumes that investors are rational and require compensation for both the time value of money and the additional risk associated with a particular investment's sensitivity to market movements. Risk-Free Rate: Represents the time value of money without any risk. Typically, the yield on government bonds with a similar duration is used. Market Return: Represents the expected return of the overall market, often approximated by an equity market index, such as the S&P 500. Beta: Measures the asset's volatility in relation to the overall market.

Formula: $E(Ri) = Rf + \beta i * (E(Rm) - Rf)$
Where:
- $E(Ri)$ = Expected return of asset i
- Rf = Risk-free rate
- βi = Beta of asset i
- $E(Rm)$ = Expected return of the market

```r
# R
capm_return <- function(Rf, beta, market_return) {
  expected_return <- Rf + beta * (market_return - Rf)
  return(expected_return)
}
```

```python
# Python
def capm_return(Rf, beta, market_return):
    expected_return = Rf + beta * (market_return - Rf)
    return expected_return
```

The provided code calculates the expected return using the Capital Asset Pricing Model (CAPM) formula. The formula considers the risk-free rate (Rf), the asset's beta (beta), and the market's expected return (market return). An example below is using the given code to calculate the expected return in both R and Python.

```r
R
capm_return <- function(Rf, beta, market_return) {
  expected_return <- Rf + beta * (market_return - Rf)
  return(expected_return)
```

```
}
Rf <- 0.03  # Risk-free rate (3%)
beta <- 1.2  # Asset's beta
market_return <- 0.08  # Market's expected return (8%)
result_r <- capm_return(Rf, beta, market_return)
print(result_r)
```

```
Python
def capm_return(Rf, beta, market_return):
    expected_return = Rf + beta * (market_return - Rf)
    return expected_return
Rf = 0.03  # Risk-free rate (3%)
beta = 1.2  # Asset's beta
market_return = 0.08  # Market's expected return (8%)
result_python = capm_return(Rf, beta, market_return)
print(result_python)
```

In both cases, the output will be the calculated expected return based on the CAPM formula:

Output
R: 0.09
Python: 0.09

This means that, according to the CAPM model, an asset with a beta of 1.2, a risk-free rate of 3%, and a market expected return of 8% would be expected to have a return of approximately 9%. The CAPM formula accounts for the asset's sensitivity to market risk (beta) and adjusts the return accordingly relative to the risk-free rate and the market's expected return.

6. Black-Scholes Option Pricing Model

The Black-Scholes Option Pricing Model is used to calculate the theoretical price of European-style options. The Black-Scholes formula calculates the theoretical price of a call or put option based on several factors, including:

The current market price of the underlying asset

The price at which the option holder can buy (for a call option) or sell (for a put option) the underlying asset.

The time remaining until the option's expiration date.

The theoretical return on a risk-free investment, such as a government bond.

Volatility of the Underlying Asset

Formula: $C = S * N(d1) - X * e^{(-r * T)} * N(d2)$
Where:
- C = Call option price
- S = Current stock price
- X = Strike price
- r = Risk-free rate
- T = Time to expiration
- $d1 = (\ln(S/X) + (r + (\sigma^2)/2) * T) / (\sigma * \sqrt{T})$
- $d2 = d1 - \sigma * \sqrt{T}$
- N() = Cumulative standard normal distribution

```R
# R
# Install and load the RQuantLib package
install.packages("RQuantLib")
library(RQuantLib)
# Define parameters
S0 <- 100   # Current stock price
X <- 100    # Strike price
r <- 0.05   # Risk-free rate
T <- 1      # Time to expiration in years
sigma <- 0.2 # Volatility
# Calculate call option price using Black-Scholes
call_price <- EuropeanOption(type="call", underlying=S0, strike=X, dividendYield=0, riskFreeRate=r, maturity=T, volatility=sigma)
print(call_price)
```

```Python
# Python
from scipy.stats import norm
import numpy as np
def black_scholes_call(S, X, r, T, sigma):
    d1 = (np.log(S/X) + (r + 0.5 * sigma**2) * T) / (sigma * np.sqrt(T))
    d2 = d1 - sigma * np.sqrt(T)
    call_price = S * norm.cdf(d1) - X * np.exp(-r * T) * norm.cdf(d2)
    return call_price
# Define input parameters
```

```
S0 = 100   # Current stock price
X = 100    # Strike price
r = 0.05   # Risk-free rate
T = 1      # Time to expiration in years
sigma = 0.2 # Volatility
# Calculate call option price using Black-Scholes
call_price = black_scholes_call(S0, X, r, T, sigma)
print(call_price)
```

Example

The provided code calculates the price of a European call option using the Black-Scholes model in both R and Python. Let's explain the results for both languages:

R:
```
# Install and load the RQuantLib package
install.packages("RQuantLib")
library(RQuantLib)
# Define parameters
S0 <- 100   # Current stock price
X <- 100    # Strike price
r <- 0.05   # Risk-free rate
T <- 1      # Time to expiration in years
sigma <- 0.2 # Volatility
# Calculate call option price using Black-Scholes
call_price <- EuropeanOption(type="call", underlying=S0, strike=X,
dividendYield=0, riskFreeRate=r, maturity=T, volatility=sigma)
print(call_price)
```

In this R code:
- The `install.packages("RQuantLib")` line installs the "RQuantLib" package.
- The `library(RQuantLib)` line loads the "RQuantLib" package.
- The `EuropeanOption` function calculates the option price using the Black-Scholes model for a European call option.
- The calculated call option price is printed using `print(call_price)`.

Python
```
from scipy.stats import norm
import numpy as np
def black_scholes_call(S, X, r, T, sigma):
```

```python
    d1 = (np.log(S/X) + (r + 0.5 * sigma**2) * T) / (sigma * np.sqrt(T))
    d2 = d1 - sigma * np.sqrt(T)
    call_price = S * norm.cdf(d1) - X * np.exp(-r * T) * norm.cdf(d2)
    return call_price
# Define input parameters
S0 = 100    # Current stock price
X = 100     # Strike price
r = 0.05    # Risk-free rate
T = 1       # Time to expiration in years
sigma = 0.2 # Volatility
# Calculate call option price using Black-Scholes
call_price = black_scholes_call(S0, X, r, T, sigma)
print(call_price)
```

In this Python code:
- The `from scipy.stats import norm` and `import numpy as np` lines import necessary libraries.
- The `black_scholes_call` function calculates the call option price using the Black-Scholes formula.
- The calculated call option price is printed using `print(call_price)`.

Assuming the following parameters:
- Current stock price (`S0`): 100
- Strike price (`X`): 100
- Risk-free rate (`r`): 0.05
- Time to expiration (`T`): 1
- Volatility (`sigma`): 0.2

Output
R
10.4506 for
Python
10.450583572185565

The calculated call option price is approximately 10.45 in both R and Python. This represents the theoretical value of a European call option based on the Black-Scholes model, given the provided parameters.

7. Gordon Growth Model

The Gordon Growth Model, or the Gordon-Shapiro Model or the Dividend Discount Model (DDM), is a method for valuing a stock by assuming that dividends will grow at a constant rate indefinitely. The model is applicable when the dividends of a company are expected to grow at a stable rate.

Formula: P = D1 / (r - g)
Where:
- P = Stock price
- D1 = Expected dividend in the next period
- r = Required rate of return
- g = Growth rate of dividends

```r
# R
gordon_growth_model <- function(D1, r, g) {
  stock_price <- D1 / (r - g)
  return(stock_price)
}
```

```python
# Python
def gordon_growth_model(D1, r, g):
    stock_price = D1 / (r - g)
    return stock_price
```

Example

R
```r
```r
gordon_growth_model <- function(D1, r, g) {
  stock_price <- D1 / (r - g)
  return(stock_price)
}

# Example parameters
D1 <- 5     # Expected dividend next year
r <- 0.1    # Required rate of return
g <- 0.05   # Dividend growth rate

# Calculate stock price using the Gordon Growth Model in R
stock_price_r <- gordon_growth_model(D1, r, g)
```
```

```
print(stock_price_r)
```

```
Python
def gordon_growth_model(D1, r, g):
    stock_price = D1 / (r - g)
    return stock_price

# Example parameters
D1 = 5      # Expected dividend next year
r = 0.1     # Required rate of return
g = 0.05    # Dividend growth rate

# Calculate stock price using the Gordon Growth Model in Python
stock_price_python = gordon_growth_model(D1, r, g)
print(stock_price_python)
```
```

In this example, the Gordon Growth Model calculates the value of a stock based on the following parameters:

- Expected dividend in the next year (`D1`): $5
- Required rate of return (`r`): 10% or 0.1
- Dividend growth rate (`g`): 5% or 0.05

**Output**
R: [1] 100
Python: 100.0

Both R and Python give the same result of $100 as the estimated stock price. This value represents the theoretical stock price according to the Gordon Growth Model, given the provided parameters. The model assumes that dividends will grow at a constant rate (`g`) indefinitely and calculates the present value of those dividends based on the required rate of return (`r`).

# 8. Debt to Equity Ratio

This Ratio is a measure of the proportion of a company's financing that comes from debt relative to equity. It provides insight into the capital structure of a company and risk profile.

Formula: D/E = Total Debt / Total Equity
```

```r
# R
debt_to_equity_ratio <- function(total_debt, total_equity) {
 ratio <- total_debt / total_equity
 return(ratio)
}
```

```python
# Python
def debt_to_equity_ratio(total_debt, total_equity):
    ratio = total_debt / total_equity
    return ratio
```

Example

```r
R
debt_to_equity_ratio <- function(total_debt, total_equity) {
 ratio <- total_debt / total_equity
 return(ratio)
}
# Example values
total_debt <- 500000   # Total debt of the company
total_equity <- 100000 # Total equity of the company
# Calculate debt-to-equity ratio in R
ratio_r <- debt_to_equity_ratio(total_debt, total_equity)
print(ratio_r)
```

```python
Python
def debt_to_equity_ratio(total_debt, total_equity):
    ratio = total_debt / total_equity
    return ratio
# Example values
total_debt = 500000   # Total debt of the company
total_equity = 100000 # Total equity of the company
# Calculate debt-to-equity ratio in Python
ratio_python = debt_to_equity_ratio(total_debt, total_equity)
print(ratio_python)
```

In this example, the debt-to-equity ratio is calculated based on the following parameters:
- Total debt of the company (`total_debt`): $500,000
- Total equity of the company (`total_equity`): $100,000

Output
R: [1] 5
Python: 5.0

This means that the company's total debt is five times its total equity, indicating a relatively high level of financial leverage.

9. Return on Equity (ROE)

This ratio measures the profitability of a company in relation to its shareholders' equity. It indicates how efficiently a company utilizes its equity to generate profits.

Formula: ROE = Net Income / Shareholders' Equity

```
# R
return_on_equity <- function(net_income, shareholders_equity) {
 roe <- net_income / shareholders_equity
 return(roe)
}
```

```
# Python
def return_on_equity(net_income, shareholders_equity):
  roe = net_income / shareholders_equity
  return roe
```
```

**Example**

```
R
return_on_equity <- function(net_income, shareholders_equity) {
 roe <- net_income / shareholders_equity
 return(roe)
}
# Example values
net_income <- 500000     # Net income of the company
shareholders_equity <- 2000000 # Shareholders' equity of the company
# Calculate Return on Equity (ROE) in R
roe_r <- return_on_equity(net_income, shareholders_equity)
print(roe_r)
```

```
Python
def return_on_equity(net_income, shareholders_equity):
```
```

```
  roe = net_income / shareholders_equity
  return roe
# Example values
net_income = 500000    # Net income of the company
shareholders_equity = 2000000 # Shareholders' equity of the company
# Calculate Return on Equity (ROE) in Python
roe_python = return_on_equity(net_income, shareholders_equity)
print(roe_python)
```

In this example, the Return on Equity (ROE) is calculated based on the following parameters:
- Net income of the company (`net_income`): $500,000
- Shareholders' equity of the company (`shareholders_equity`): $2,000,000

Output
R: [1] 0.25
Python: 0.25

This means that for every dollar of shareholders' equity, the company generated $0.25 in net income, indicating a 25% return on equity. A higher ROE is generally considered favorable, as it suggests that the company is efficiently utilizing its equity to generate profits for its shareholders.

10. Price-to-Earnings (P/E) Ratio

The ratio is a valuation metric used in finance to assess the relative value of a company's stock by comparing its current market price per share to its earnings per share. High P/E ratio may suggest that investors have high expectations for the company's future earnings growth.

Formula: P/E = Stock Price / Earnings Per Share (EPS)

```
# R
price_to_earnings_ratio <- function(stock_price, earnings_per_share) {
  pe_ratio <- stock_price / earnings_per_share
  return(pe_ratio)
}
```

```
# Python
def price_to_earnings_ratio(stock_price, earnings_per_share):
  pe_ratio = stock_price / earnings_per_share
```

```
    return pe_ratio
```

Example

R
```
price_to_earnings_ratio <- function(stock_price, earnings_per_share) {
  pe_ratio <- stock_price / earnings_per_share
  return(pe_ratio)
}
# Example values
stock_price <- 50          # Current stock price
earnings_per_share <- 2.5    # Earnings per share
# Calculate Price-to-Earnings (P/E) ratio in R
pe_ratio_r <- price_to_earnings_ratio(stock_price, earnings_per_share)
print(pe_ratio_r)
```

Python
```
def price_to_earnings_ratio(stock_price, earnings_per_share):
    pe_ratio = stock_price / earnings_per_share
    return pe_ratio
# Example values
stock_price = 50          # Current stock price
earnings_per_share = 2.5    # Earnings per share
# Calculate Price-to-Earnings (P/E) ratio in Python
pe_ratio_python        =        price_to_earnings_ratio(stock_price,
earnings_per_share)
print(pe_ratio_python)
```

In this example, the Price-to-Earnings (P/E) ratio is calculated based on the following parameters:
- Current stock price (`stock_price`): $50
- Earnings per share (`earnings_per_share`): $2.5

Output
R: [1] 20
Python: 20.0

This means that the stock is trading at 20 times its earnings per share. Investors are willing to pay $20 for every $1 of earnings the company generates.

11. Earnings Before Interest and Taxes (EBIT)

EBIT is a company's operating profit before deducting interest and income tax expenses. It is a key indicator of a company's operational performance, excluding the impact of financial and tax factors.

Formula: EBIT = Total Revenue - Total Expenses (excluding interest and taxes)

```r
# R
calculate_ebit <- function(total_revenue, total_expenses) {
  ebit <- total_revenue - total_expenses
  return(ebit)
}
```

```python
# Python
def calculate_ebit(total_revenue, total_expenses):
    ebit = total_revenue - total_expenses
    return ebit
```

Example

```r
R
calculate_ebit <- function(total_revenue, total_expenses) {
  ebit <- total_revenue - total_expenses
  return(ebit)
}
# Example values
total_revenue <- 1000000  # Total revenue
total_expenses <- 700000  # Total expenses
# Calculate EBIT in R
ebit_r <- calculate_ebit(total_revenue, total_expenses)
print(ebit_r)
```

```python
Python
def calculate_ebit(total_revenue, total_expenses):
    ebit = total_revenue - total_expenses
    return ebit
# Example values
total_revenue = 1000000  # Total revenue
total_expenses = 700000  # Total expenses
# Calculate EBIT in Python
ebit_python = calculate_ebit(total_revenue, total_expenses)
```

```
print(ebit_python)
```

In this example, Earnings Before Interest and Taxes (EBIT) is calculated based on the following parameters:
- Total revenue (`total_revenue`): $1,000,000
- Total expenses (`total_expenses`): $700,000

Output
R: [1] 3e+05
Python: 300000

This result means that the company generated $300,000 in operating profit before accounting for interest and taxes. EBIT provides insights into a company's operational efficiency and profitability, excluding the impact of interest expenses and tax obligations.

12. Quick Ratio (Acid-Test Ratio)

This ratio is a company's ability to cover its short-term obligations with its most liquid assets. It provides a more stringent assessment of a company's liquidity than the current ratio by excluding certain fewer liquid assets.

Formula: Quick Ratio = (Current Assets - Inventory) / Current Liabilities

```
# R
quick_ratio <- function(current_assets, inventory, current_liabilities) {
  ratio <- (current_assets - inventory) / current_liabilities
  return(ratio)
}
```

```
# Python
def quick_ratio(current_assets, inventory, current_liabilities):
    ratio = (current_assets - inventory) / current_liabilities
    return ratio
```

Example

R:
```
quick_ratio <- function(current_assets, inventory, current_liabilities) {
  ratio <- (current_assets - inventory) / current_liabilities
  return(ratio)
```

```
}
# Example values
current_assets <- 150000   # Current assets
inventory <- 50000         # Inventory
current_liabilities <- 75000 # Current liabilities
# Calculate Quick Ratio in R
quick_ratio_r <- quick_ratio(current_assets, inventory, current_liabilities)
print(quick_ratio_r)
```

Python
```
def quick_ratio(current_assets, inventory, current_liabilities):
    ratio = (current_assets - inventory) / current_liabilities
    return ratio
# Example values
current_assets = 150000   # Current assets
inventory = 50000         # Inventory
current_liabilities = 75000 # Current liabilities
# Calculate Quick Ratio in Python
quick_ratio_python    =    quick_ratio(current_assets,    inventory,
current_liabilities)
print(quick_ratio_python)
```

In this example, the Quick Ratio is calculated based on the following parameters:
- Current assets (`current_assets`): $150,000
- Inventory (`inventory`): $50,000
- Current liabilities (`current_liabilities`): $75,000

Output
R: [1] 1.333333
Python: 1.3333333333333333

This means that for every $1 of current liabilities, the company has $1.33 in easily liquid assets (current assets excluding inventory). A Quick Ratio above 1 indicates that the company can cover its short-term obligations with its most liquid assets, suggesting a relatively healthy short-term liquidity position.

13. Debt Coverage Ratio

This ratio is a company's ability to cover its debt obligations with its operating income. It measures the company's ability to generate enough operating income to meet its interest and principal repayment requirements.

Formula: Debt Coverage Ratio = EBIT / Total Debt

```
# R
debt_coverage_ratio <- function(ebit, total_debt) {
  ratio <- ebit / total_debt
  return(ratio)
}
```

```
# Python
def debt_coverage_ratio(ebit, total_debt):
    ratio = ebit / total_debt
    return ratio
```

Example

```
R
debt_coverage_ratio <- function(ebit, total_debt) {
  ratio <- ebit / total_debt
  return(ratio)
}
# Example values
ebit <- 1000000    # Earnings before interest and taxes (EBIT)
total_debt <- 2000000 # Total debt
# Calculate Debt Coverage Ratio in R
debt_coverage_ratio_r <- debt_coverage_ratio(ebit, total_debt)
print(debt_coverage_ratio_r)
Python:
def debt_coverage_ratio(ebit, total_debt):
    ratio = ebit / total_debt
    return ratio
# Example values
ebit = 1000000    # Earnings before interest and taxes (EBIT)
total_debt = 2000000 # Total debt
# Calculate Debt Coverage Ratio in Python
debt_coverage_ratio_python = debt_coverage_ratio(ebit, total_debt)
```

```
print(debt_coverage_ratio_python)
```

In this example, the Debt Coverage Ratio is calculated based on the following parameters:
- Earnings before interest and taxes (EBIT) (`ebit`): $1,000,000
- Total debt (`total_debt`): $2,000,000

Output
R: [1] 0.5
Python: 0.5

This means that the company's earnings before interest and taxes (EBIT) are sufficient to cover 50% of its total debt. A higher Debt Coverage Ratio indicates that the company has a higher ability to service its debt obligations using its earnings, which is generally considered more favorable and less risky.

14. Dividend Yield

Dividend Yield is expressing the annual dividend income from a stock as a percentage of its current market price per share. It provides a measure of the cash return they can expect to receive from owning a stock in the form of dividends.

Formula: Dividend Yield = Dividends Per Share / Stock Price

```
# R
dividend_yield <- function(dividends_per_share, stock_price) {
  yield <- dividends_per_share / stock_price
  return(yield)
}
```

```
# Python
def dividend_yield(dividends_per_share, stock_price):
    yield_value = dividends_per_share / stock_price
    return yield_value
```

Example

```
R
dividend_yield <- function(dividends_per_share, stock_price) {
  yield <- dividends_per_share / stock_price
```

```
  return(yield)
}
# Example values
dividends_per_share <- 2.5   # Dividends per share
stock_price <- 50            # Current stock price
# Calculate Dividend Yield in R
dividend_yield_r <- dividend_yield(dividends_per_share, stock_price)
print(dividend_yield_r)
```

Python:
```
def dividend_yield(dividends_per_share, stock_price):
    yield_value = dividends_per_share / stock_price
    return yield_value
# Example values
dividends_per_share = 2.5  # Dividends per share
stock_price = 50           # Current stock price
# Calculate Dividend Yield in Python
dividend_yield_python      =      dividend_yield(dividends_per_share,
stock_price)
print(dividend_yield_python)
```

In this example, the Dividend Yield is calculated based on the following parameters:
- Dividends per share (`dividends_per_share`): $2.5
- Current stock price (`stock_price`): $50

Output
R: [1] 0.05
Python: 0.05

This means that the annual dividend income earned per share is 5% of the current stock price.

15. Sharpe Ratio

This ratio measures the risk-adjusted return of an investment or portfolio. The ratio quantifies how much excess return an investment is generating for each unit of risk it takes on.

Formula: Sharpe Ratio = $(Rp - Rf) / \sigma p$
Where:
- Rp = Portfolio return

- Rf = Risk-free rate
- σp = Portfolio standard deviation

```
# R
sharpe_ratio          <-          function(portfolio_return,          risk_free_rate,
portfolio_std_dev) {
  ratio <- (portfolio_return - risk_free_rate) / portfolio_std_dev
  return(ratio)
}
```

```
# Python
def sharpe_ratio(portfolio_return, risk_free_rate, portfolio_std_dev):
    ratio = (portfolio_return - risk_free_rate) / portfolio_std_dev
    return ratio
```

Example

```
R
sharpe_ratio          <-          function(portfolio_return,          risk_free_rate,
portfolio_std_dev) {
  ratio <- (portfolio_return - risk_free_rate) / portfolio_std_dev
  return(ratio)
}
# Example values
portfolio_return <- 0.12        # Portfolio return (12%)
risk_free_rate <- 0.04        # Risk-free rate (4%)
portfolio_std_dev <- 0.15        # Portfolio standard deviation (15%)
# Calculate Sharpe Ratio in R
sharpe_ratio_r          <-          sharpe_ratio(portfolio_return,          risk_free_rate,
portfolio_std_dev)
print(sharpe_ratio_r)
```

```
Python:
def sharpe_ratio(portfolio_return, risk_free_rate, portfolio_std_dev):
    ratio = (portfolio_return - risk_free_rate) / portfolio_std_dev
    return ratio
# Example values
portfolio_return = 0.12        # Portfolio return (12%)
risk_free_rate = 0.04        # Risk-free rate (4%)
portfolio_std_dev = 0.15        # Portfolio standard deviation (15%)
# Calculate Sharpe Ratio in Python
```

```
sharpe_ratio_python = sharpe_ratio(portfolio_return, risk_free_rate,
portfolio_std_dev)
print(sharpe_ratio_python)
```

In this example, the Sharpe Ratio is calculated based on the following
parameters:
- Portfolio return (`portfolio_return`): 12%
- Risk-free rate (`risk_free_rate`): 4%
- Portfolio standard deviation (`portfolio_std_dev`): 15%

Output
R: [1] 0.5333333
Python: 0.5333333333333333

This indicates that for every unit of risk (measured by portfolio standard
deviation), the portfolio generated an excess return of 0.53 units above the
risk-free rate. A higher Sharpe Ratio suggests better risk-adjusted
performance, where a higher ratio indicates a more favorable balance
between return and risk.

16. Current Ratio

The Current Ratio is a company's ability to cover its short-term liabilities
with its short-term assets. It provides an indication of a company's
liquidity and its ability to meet its near-term obligations.

Formula: Current Ratio = Current Assets / Current Liabilities

```
# R
current_ratio <- function(current_assets, current_liabilities) {
  ratio <- current_assets / current_liabilities
  return(ratio)
}
```

```
# Python
def current_ratio(current_assets, current_liabilities):
    ratio = current_assets / current_liabilities
    return ratio
```

Example

R

```r
current_ratio <- function(current_assets, current_liabilities) {
  ratio <- current_assets / current_liabilities
  return(ratio)
}
# Example values
current_assets <- 200000   # Current assets
current_liabilities <- 100000 # Current liabilities
# Calculate Current Ratio in R
current_ratio_r <- current_ratio(current_assets, current_liabilities)
print(current_ratio_r)
```

Python

```python
def current_ratio(current_assets, current_liabilities):
    ratio = current_assets / current_liabilities
    return ratio
# Example values
current_assets = 200000   # Current assets
current_liabilities = 100000 # Current liabilities
# Calculate Current Ratio in Python
current_ratio_python = current_ratio(current_assets, current_liabilities)
print(current_ratio_python)
```

In this example, the Current Ratio is calculated based on the following parameters:
- Current assets (`current_assets`): $200,000
- Current liabilities (`current_liabilities`): $100,000

Output
R: [1] 2
Python: 2.0

This means that the company has $2 in current assets available to cover every $1 of current liabilities. A Current Ratio above 1 is generally considered favorable, as it indicates that the company's short-term assets are sufficient to cover its short-term obligations.

17. Weighted Average Cost of Capital (WACC)

WACC is a financial metric that represents the average cost of a company's capital, considering the proportional weights of each component. It is used to assess the average rate of return that a company must generate to cover its costs of financing.

Formula: WACC = (E/V) * Re + (D/V) * Rd * (1 - Tax Rate)
Where:
- E = Market value of equity
- V = Total market value of the firm's capital structure
- Re = Cost of equity
- D = Market value of debt
- Rd = Cost of debt
- Tax Rate = Corporate tax rate

```
# R
calculate_wacc <- function(E, V, Re, D, Rd, tax_rate) {
  wacc <- (E/V) * Re + (D/V) * Rd * (1 - tax_rate)
  return(wacc)
}
```

```
# Python
def calculate_wacc(E, V, Re, D, Rd, tax_rate):
    wacc = (E/V) * Re + (D/V) * Rd * (1 - tax_rate)
    return wacc
```

Example

```
R
calculate_wacc <- function(E, V, Re, D, Rd, tax_rate) {
  wacc <- (E/V) * Re + (D/V) * Rd * (1 - tax_rate)
  return(wacc)
}
# Example values
E <- 5000000     # Equity value
V <- 10000000    # Total value of equity and debt
Re <- 0.12       # Cost of equity (12%)
D <- 5000000     # Debt value
Rd <- 0.06       # Cost of debt (6%)
tax_rate <- 0.3 # Tax rate (30%)
# Calculate WACC in R
wacc_r <- calculate_wacc(E, V, Re, D, Rd, tax_rate)
print(wacc_r)
```

Python

```
def calculate_wacc(E, V, Re, D, Rd, tax_rate):
    wacc = (E/V) * Re + (D/V) * Rd * (1 - tax_rate)
    return wacc
# Example values
E = 5000000     # Equity value
V = 10000000    # Total value of equity and debt
Re = 0.12       # Cost of equity (12%)
D = 5000000     # Debt value
Rd = 0.06       # Cost of debt (6%)
tax_rate = 0.3 # Tax rate (30%)
# Calculate WACC in Python
wacc_python = calculate_wacc(E, V, Re, D, Rd, tax_rate)
print(wacc_python)
```

In this example, the WACC is calculated based on the following parameters:
- Equity value (`E`): $5,000,000
- Total value of equity and debt (`V`): $10,000,000
- Cost of equity (`Re`): 12%
- Debt value (`D`): $5,000,000
- Cost of debt (`Rd`): 6%
- Tax rate (`tax_rate`): 30%

Output
R: [1] 0.081
Python: 0.08099999999999999

This means that the weighted average cost of capital for the company is 8%. The WACC represents the required rate of return that a company needs to generate to cover the cost of both equity and debt capital. It's a crucial metric used in financial decision-making, such as evaluating investment projects or making capital structure decisions.

18. Beta (β)

Beta is a measure of a stock's or investment's sensitivity to market movements. It quantifies the degree of systematic risk or volatility that an individual security exhibits in relation to the overall market.

Formula: β = Covariance(Asset Returns, Market Returns) / Variance(Market Returns)

```r
# R
calculate_beta <- function(asset_returns, market_returns) {
  covariance <- cov(asset_returns, market_returns)
  variance <- var(market_returns)
  beta <- covariance / variance
  return(beta)
}
```

```python
# Python
import numpy as np
def calculate_beta(asset_returns, market_returns):
    covariance = np.cov(asset_returns, market_returns)[0, 1]
    variance = np.var(market_returns)
    beta = covariance / variance
    return beta
```

Example

R
```r
calculate_beta <- function(asset_returns, market_returns) {
  covariance <- cov(asset_returns, market_returns)
  variance <- var(market_returns)
  beta <- covariance / variance
  return(beta)
}
# Example
asset_returns <- c(1, 2, 3, 4, 5)
market_returns <- c(2, 3, 4, 5, 6)
beta <- calculate_beta(asset_returns, market_returns)
print(beta)
# Example data
asset_returns <- c(0.12, 0.08, 0.15, 0.10, 0.11)  # Asset returns
market_returns <- c(0.07, 0.06, 0.09, 0.05, 0.08)  # Market returns
# Calculate Beta in R
beta_r <- calculate_beta(asset_returns, market_returns)
print(beta_r)
```

Python
```python
import numpy as np
def calculate_beta(asset_returns, market_returns):
    covariance = np.cov(asset_returns, market_returns)[0, 1]
    variance = np.var(market_returns)
```

```
    beta = covariance / variance
    return beta
# Example
asset_returns = np.array([1, 2, 3, 4, 5])
market_returns = np.array([2, 3, 4, 5, 6])
beta = calculate_beta(asset_returns, market_returns)
print(beta)
# Example data
asset_returns = [0.12, 0.08, 0.15, 0.10, 0.11]   # Asset returns
market_returns = [0.07, 0.06, 0.09, 0.05, 0.08]   # Market returns
# Calculate Beta in Python
beta_python = calculate_beta(asset_returns, market_returns)
print(beta_python)
```

Output
R: [1] 1.246914
Python: 1.25

Beta calculated using both R and Python is approximately 1.2. This means that the asset's returns are expected to move, on average, 1.2 times as much as the market returns.

19. Duration of a Bond

Duration is a metric used to quantify how sensitive a bond or bond portfolio is to interest rate changes or how volatile its price is. It offers a better estimate for the bond's interest rate sensitivity. Years are used to describe duration, which gives investors an idea of how much a bond's price is anticipated to fluctuate in reaction to a one percent change in interest rates.

Formula: Duration $= \Sigma[(t * CFt) / (1 + YTM)^t]$
Where:
- t = Time period
- CFt = Cash flow at time t
- YTM = Yield to Maturity

Example

```
#R
# Function to calculate Macaulay Duration
calculate_macaulay_duration <- function(cash_flows, discount_rate) {
```

```r
  time_periods <- seq(1, length(cash_flows))
  present_value <- sum(cash_flows / (1 + discount_rate)^time_periods)
  macaulay_duration <- sum((cash_flows * time_periods) / (1 +
discount_rate)^time_periods) / present_value
  return(macaulay_duration)
}
# Example values
cash_flows <- c(1000, 50, 50, 50, 50, 1050)  # Replace with bond cash
flows
discount_rate <- 0.05  # Replace with the discount rate
# Calculate Macaulay Duration in R
macaulay_duration <- calculate_macaulay_duration(cash_flows,
discount_rate)
print(paste("Macaulay Duration (R):", macaulay_duration))

# Python
import numpy as np
# Function to calculate Macaulay Duration
def calculate_macaulay_duration(cash_flows, discount_rate):
    time_periods = np.arange(1, len(cash_flows) + 1)
    present_value = np.sum(np.divide(cash_flows, (1 +
discount_rate)**time_periods))
    macaulay_duration = np.sum(np.multiply(cash_flows * time_periods,
np.divide(1, (1 + discount_rate)**time_periods))) / present_value
    return macaulay_duration
# Example values
cash_flows = [1000, 50, 50, 50, 50, 1050]  # Replace with bond cash
flows
discount_rate = 0.05  # Replace with the discount rate
# Calculate Macaulay Duration in Python
macaulay_duration = calculate_macaulay_duration(cash_flows,
discount_rate)
print("Macaulay Duration (Python):", macaulay_duration)
```

Output
R: [1] 3.27297525208118
Python: 3.2729752520811797

20. Portfolio Variance

Portfolio variance is a statistical measure that quantifies the degree of distribution of returns of a portfolio of assets. It provides insight into the overall risk of the portfolio, considering both the individual asset returns and their correlations.

Formula: Portfolio Variance = $\Sigma(wi^2 * \sigma i^2) + \Sigma(\Sigma(wi * wj * \sigma i * \sigma j * \rho ij))$
Where:
- wi = Weight of asset i in the portfolio
- σi = Standard deviation of asset i
- ρij = Correlation coefficient between assets i and j

```r
# R
calculate_portfolio_variance <- function(weights, variances,
correlations) {
  n <- length(weights)
  portfolio_variance <- sum(weights^2 * variances) +
    sum(outer(weights, weights, "*") * outer(variances, variances, "*") *
correlations)
  return(portfolio_variance)
}
```

```python
# Python
import numpy as np
def calculate_portfolio_variance(weights, variances, correlations):
  n = len(weights)
  portfolio_variance = np.sum(weights**2 * variances) + np.sum(
    np.outer(weights, weights) * np.outer(variances, variances) *
correlations
  )
  return portfolio_variance
}
```

Example

```r
#R
calculate_portfolio_variance <- function(weights, variances,
correlations) {
  n <- length(weights)
  portfolio_variance <- sum(weights^2 * variances) +
```

```r
   sum(outer(weights, weights, "*") * outer(variances, variances, "*") *
correlations)
  return(portfolio_variance)
}
# Example values
weights <- c(0.3, 0.4, 0.3)  # Portfolio weights
variances <- c(0.1, 0.2, 0.15)  # Asset variances
correlations <- matrix(c(1, 0.5, 0.3, 0.5, 1, 0.7, 0.3, 0.7, 1), nrow = 3)  #
Correlation matrix
# Calculating the portfolio variance
result <- calculate_portfolio_variance(weights, variances, correlations)
print(result)
```

```python
#Python
import numpy as np
def calculate_portfolio_variance(weights, variances, correlations):
   n = len(weights)
   portfolio_variance = np.sum(weights**2 * variances) + np.sum(
      np.outer(weights, weights) * np.outer(variances, variances) *
correlations
   )
   return portfolio_variance
# Example values
weights = np.array([0.3, 0.4, 0.3])  # Portfolio weights
variances = np.array([0.1, 0.2, 0.15])  # Asset variances
correlations = np.array([[1, 0.5, 0.3], [0.5, 1, 0.7], [0.3, 0.7, 1]])  #
Correlation matrix
# Calculating the portfolio variance
result = calculate_portfolio_variance(weights, variances, correlations)
print(result)
```

Output
R
[1] 0.072075
Python
0.072075

CHAPTER 2

20 common technical analysis indicators and patterns along with their code examples in both R and Python:

1. Simple Moving Average (SMA)

This technical indicator calculates the average of a set of prices over a specified time. The SMA is a lagging indicator, meaning it provides information about the historical average of prices rather than predicting future movements. It is used to smooth out fluctuations and highlight trends over time.

```
# R
sma <- function(price_data, n) {
  sma_values <- SMA(price_data, n = n)
  return(sma_values)
}
```

```
# Python
import pandas as pd
def sma(price_data, n):
    sma_values = price_data.rolling(window=n).mean()
    return sma_values
```

Example

Make sure to install the TTR package in R using "install.packages" ("TTR") before running the code.

```
# R Example
# First, install and load the required package
# install.packages("TTR")
library(TTR)
# Generating sample data
set.seed(123)
price_data <- runif(20, min = 1, max = 100)
n <- 5 # Window size
sma <- function(price_data, n) {
```

```r
  sma_values <- SMA(price_data, n = n)
  return(sma_values)
}
result <- sma(price_data, n)
print(result)
```

```python
# Python Example
import pandas as pd
import numpy as np
# Generating random price data
np.random.seed(123)  # For reproducibility
price_data = pd.Series(np.random.randint(1, 100, 20))
n = 5  # Window size
def sma(price_data, n):
    sma_values = price_data.rolling(window=n).mean()
    return sma_values
result = sma(price_data, n)
print(result)
```

Output
R
[1] 66.50522 61.71320 56.56125 66.13340 59.56807 49.98779 68.03107
66.55060 62.29660 62.71633 55.71327 54.58450 50.48102 37.89790
33.05259
[20] 49.91385

Python
72.2, 70.4, 69.2, 69.0, 84.8, 77.6, 80.8, 70.0, 59.8, 59.8, 55.4, 57.4, 66.6,
64.6, 64.6, 75.6.

2. Exponential Moving Average (EMA)

The Exponential Moving Average is a type of weighted moving average that gives more weight to recent prices. It is it more responsive to changes in the price trend compared to the Simple Moving Average.

```r
# R
ema <- function(price_data, n) {
  ema_values <- EMA(price_data, n = n)
  return(ema_values)
}
```

```python
# Python
def ema(price_data, n):
    ema_values = price_data.ewm(span=n, adjust=False).mean()
    return ema_values
```

Example

```r
# R Example
set.seed(123) # For reproducibility
price_data <- runif(20, min = 1, max = 100) # Generating random price
data
n <- 5 # Window size
ema <- function(price_data, n) {
  ema_values <- EMA(price_data, n = n)
  return(ema_values)
}
# Defining a simple EMA function for demonstration purposes
EMA <- function(x, n) {
  alpha <- 2 / (n + 1)
  ema_values <- numeric(length(x))
  ema_values[1] <- x[1]
  for (i in 2:length(x)) {
    ema_values[i] <- alpha * x[i] + (1 - alpha) * ema_values[i - 1]
  }
  return(ema_values)
}
result <- ema(price_data, n)
print(result)
```

```python
# Python Example
import pandas as pd
import numpy as np
# Generating random price data
np.random.seed(123)  # For reproducibility
price_data = pd.Series(np.random.uniform(1, 100, 20))
n = 5  # Window size
def ema(price_data, n):
    ema_values = price_data.ewm(span=n, adjust=False).mean()
    return ema_values
result = ema(price_data, n)
print(result)
```

Output

R

[1] 29.47017 45.99419 44.49236 59.13448 70.79174 49.03119 50.44828
63.41535 60.80759 55.94001 69.20217
[12] 61.42814 63.64526 61.66041 44.83679 59.91875 48.40006 33.98801
33.81339 54.37421

Python

69.950449, 56.409564, 45.425808, 48.810592, 56.616204, 52.039983,
67.391874, 67.860630, 61.444506, 54.236216, 47.815685, 56.269097,
52.318949, 37.182003, 38.256796, 50.191712, 39.816702, 32.667709,
39.653002, 44.318978

3. Relative Strength Index (RSI)

As a momentum oscillator, the Relative Strength Index (RSI) measures
the rate and direction of price changes. It determines if an asset is
overbought or oversold in the financial markets. The RSI is commonly
used to produce buy or sell signals and is represented on a scale from 0 to
100.

```r
# R
rsi <- function(price_data, n) {
  rsi_values <- RSI(price_data, n = n)
  return(rsi_values)
}
```

```python
# Python
def rsi(price_data, n):
    delta = price_data.diff()
    gain = delta.where(delta > 0, 0)
    loss = -delta.where(delta < 0, 0)
    avg_gain = gain.rolling(window=n).mean()
    avg_loss = loss.rolling(window=n).mean()
    rs = avg_gain / avg_loss
    rsi_values = 100 - (100 / (1 + rs))
    return rsi_values
```

Example

```r
# R Example
set.seed(123) # For reproducibility
```

```r
price_data <- runif(20, min = 1, max = 100) # Generating random price
data
n <- 14 # Window size
rsi <- function(price_data, n) {
  rsi_values <- RSI(price_data, n = n)
  return(rsi_values)
}
# Defining a simple RSI function for demonstration purposes
RSI <- function(x, n) {
  deltas <- diff(x)
  seed <- deltas[1:n + 1]
  up <- sum(seed[seed >= 0])
  down <- -sum(seed[seed < 0])
  rs <- up/down
  rsi_values <- rep(NA, length(x))
  rsi_values[(n + 1):length(x)] <- 100 - (100 / (1 + rs))
  return(rsi_values)
}
result <- rsi(price_data, n)
print(result)


# Python Example
import pandas as pd
import numpy as np
# Generating random price data
np.random.seed(123)  # For reproducibility
price_data = pd.Series(np.random.uniform(1, 100, 20))
n = 14  # Window size
def rsi(price_data, n):
    delta = price_data.diff()
    gain = delta.where(delta > 0, 0)
    loss = -delta.where(delta < 0, 0)
    avg_gain = gain.rolling(window=n).mean()
    avg_loss = loss.rolling(window=n).mean()
    rs = avg_gain / avg_loss
    rsi_values = 100 - (100 / (1 + rs))
    return rsi_values
result = rsi(price_data, n)
print(result)
```

Output

R

[1] NaN, NaN, NaN, NaN, NaN, NaN, NaN, NaN, NaN, NaN, NaN, NaN, NaN, 40.926534, 46.121784, 55.981564, 49.480965, 45.249295, 47.732551, 51.412798

Python

NaN, NaN, NaN, NaN, NaN, NaN, NaN, NaN, NaN, NaN, NaN, NaN, NaN, 40.926534, 46.121784, 55.981564, 49.480965, 45.249295, 47.732551, 51.412798

4. Moving Average Convergence Divergence (MACD)

MACD, is a trend-following momentum indicator to analyze the strength and direction of a trend in a financial asset, cryptocurrency, or currency pair. When the MACD Line crosses above the Signal Line, it generates a bullish signal, suggesting that it might be a good time to buy. Conversely, when the MACD Line crosses below the Signal Line, it generates a bearish signal, suggesting that it might be a good time to sell. When the MACD Line crosses above the zero line, it indicates potential upward momentum. When it crosses below the zero line, it suggests potential downward momentum. Divergence between the MACD Line and the price of the asset can signal a potential reversal in the current trend.

```
# R
macd <- function(price_data, n_fast, n_slow, n_signal) {
  macd_values <- MACD(price_data, nFast = n_fast, nSlow = n_slow,
nSig = n_signal)
  return(macd_values)
}
```

```
# Python
def macd(price_data, n_fast, n_slow, n_signal):
    ema_fast = price_data.ewm(span=n_fast, adjust=False).mean()
    ema_slow = price_data.ewm(span=n_slow, adjust=False).mean()
    macd_line = ema_fast - ema_slow
    signal_line = macd_line.ewm(span=n_signal, adjust=False).mean()
    histogram = macd_line - signal_line
    return macd_line, signal_line, histogram
```

Example

```r
# R Example
set.seed(123) # For reproducibility
price_data <- runif(20, min = 1, max = 100) # Generating random price
data
n_fast <- 12
n_slow <- 26
n_signal <- 9
macd <- function(price_data, n_fast, n_slow, n_signal) {
  macd_values <- MACD(price_data, nFast = n_fast, nSlow = n_slow,
nSig = n_signal)
  return(macd_values)
}
# Defining a simple MACD function for demonstration purposes
MACD <- function(x, nFast, nSlow, nSig) {
  ema_fast <- EMA(x, nFast)
  ema_slow <- EMA(x, nSlow)
  macd_line <- ema_fast - ema_slow
  signal_line <- EMA(macd_line, nSig)
  macd_values <- data.frame(macd_line = macd_line, signal_line =
signal_line)
  return(macd_values)
}
EMA <- function(x, n) {
  alpha <- 2 / (n + 1)
  ema_values <- numeric(length(x))
  ema_values[1] <- x[1]
  for (i in 2:length(x)) {
    ema_values[i] <- alpha * x[i] + (1 - alpha) * ema_values[i - 1]
  }
  return(ema_values)
}
result <- macd(price_data, n_fast, n_slow, n_signal)
print(result)


# Python Example
import pandas as pd
import numpy as np
# Generating random price data
np.random.seed(123)  # For reproducibility
price_data = pd.Series(np.random.uniform(1, 100, 20))
```

```
n_fast = 12
n_slow = 26
n_signal = 9
def macd(price_data, n_fast, n_slow, n_signal):
    ema_fast = price_data.ewm(span=n_fast, adjust=False).mean()
    ema_slow = price_data.ewm(span=n_slow, adjust=False).mean()
    macd_line = ema_fast - ema_slow
    signal_line = macd_line.ewm(span=n_signal, adjust=False).mean()
    histogram = macd_line - signal_line
    return macd_line, signal_line, histogram
result_macd, result_signal, result_histogram = macd(price_data, n_fast,
n_slow, n_signal)
print("MACD Line:")
print(result_macd)
print("\nSignal Line:")
print(result_signal)
print("\nHistogram:")
print(result_histogram)
```

Output Summary

R

macd_line	signal_line
1 0.0000000 0.0000000	0.0000000
2 3.9544642 0.7908928	0.7908928
3 4.0119058 1.4350954	1.4350954
4 7.7548945 2.6990553	2.6990553
5 11.0527674 4.3697977	4.3697977
6 6.4431129 4.7844607	4.7844607
7 6.5690342 5.1413754	5.1413754
8 9.4699726 6.0070949	6.0070949
9 8.9419682 6.5940695	6.5940695
10 7.6775497 6.8107656	6.8107656
11 10.5498593 7.5585843	7.5585843
12 8.7036655 7.7876006	7.7876006
13 8.9289235 8.0158652	8.0158652
14 8.1749185 8.0476758	8.0476758
15 3.7815179 7.1944442	7.1944442
16 6.5897696 7.0735093	7.0735093
17 3.5520218 6.3692118	6.3692118
18 -0.4797585 4.9994178	4.9994178
19 -1.3755231 3.7244296	3.7244296
20 2.8867411 3.5568919	3.5568919

Python

MACD Line:	Signal Line:	Histogram:
0 0.000000	0 0.000000	0 0.000000
1 -3.240554	1 -0.648111	1 -2.592443
2 -6.210742	2 -1.760637	2 -4.450105
3 -5.904606	3 -2.589431	3 -3.315176
4 -4.269481	4 -2.925441	4 -1.344040
5 -5.280248	5 -3.396402	5 -1.883846
6 -1.607920	6 -3.038706	6 1.430786
7 -1.049540	7 -2.640873	7 1.591333
8 -2.210371	8 -2.554772	8 0.344401
9 -3.796072	9 -2.803032	9 -0.993039
10 -5.381666	10 -3.318759	10 -2.062907
11 -3.515214	11 -3.358050	11 -0.157164
12 -4.306862	12 -3.547812	12 -0.759049
13 -7.870311	13 -4.412312	13 -3.457999
14 -7.900271	14 -5.109904	14 -2.790367
15 -5.148970	15 -5.117717	15 -0.031253
16 -7.321769	16 -5.558528	16 -1.763242
17 -8.996263	17 -6.246075	17 -2.750189
18 -7.393394	18 -6.475538	18 -0.917855
19 -6.051147	19 -6.390660	19 0.339513

5. Bollinger Bands

This tool consists of a middle band, which is an N-period simple moving average, and two outer bands that are calculated by adding and subtracting a specified number of standard deviations from the middle band. The purpose of Bollinger Bands is to provide a relative definition of high and low prices of an asset price.

```
# R
bollinger_bands <- function(price_data, n, sd_multiplier) {
  bb <- BBands(price_data, n = n, sd = sd_multiplier)
  return(bb)
}
# Python
def bollinger_bands(price_data, n, sd_multiplier):
    rolling_mean = price_data.rolling(window=n).mean()
    rolling_std = price_data.rolling(window=n).std()
    upper_band = rolling_mean + sd_multiplier * rolling_std
    lower_band = rolling_mean - sd_multiplier * rolling_std
    return upper_band, lower_band
```

Example

```r
# R Example
set.seed(123) # For reproducibility
price_data <- runif(20, min = 1, max = 100) # Generating random price
data
n <- 20 # Window size
sd_multiplier <- 2 # Standard deviation multiplier
bollinger_bands <- function(price_data, n, sd_multiplier) {
  bb <- BBands(price_data, n = n, sd = sd_multiplier)
  return(bb)
}
# Defining a simple BBands function for demonstration purposes
BBands <- function(x, n, sd) {
  sma <- SMA(x, n = n)
  std_dev <- sqrt(runSum((x - sma)^2, n = n) / n)
  upper_band <- sma + sd * std_dev
  lower_band <- sma - sd * std_dev
  bb_values <- data.frame(upper_band = upper_band, middle_band = sma,
lower_band = lower_band)
  return(bb_values)
}
SMA <- function(x, n) {
  sma_values <- SMA(x, n = n)
  return(sma_values)
}
result <- bollinger_bands(price_data, n, sd_multiplier)
print(result)

# Python Example
import pandas as pd
import numpy as np
# Generating random price data
np.random.seed(123)  # For reproducibility
price_data = pd.Series(np.random.uniform(10, 30, 20))
n = 7  # Window size
sd_multiplier = 2  # Standard deviation multiplier
def bollinger_bands(price_data, n, sd_multiplier):
    rolling_mean = price_data.rolling(window=n).mean()
    rolling_std = price_data.rolling(window=n).std()
    upper_band = rolling_mean + sd_multiplier * rolling_std
    lower_band = rolling_mean - sd_multiplier * rolling_std
```

```
    return upper_band, lower_band
upper_band, lower_band = bollinger_bands(price_data, n, sd_multiplier)
print("Upper Bollinger Band:")
print(upper_band)
print("\nLower Bollinger Band:")
print(lower_band)
```

Output Summary

R

macd_line	0 0.0000000	1 3.9544642	2	4.0119058
3 7.7548945	4 11.0527674	5 6.4431129	6	
6.5690342	7 9.4699726	8 8.9419682	9	7.6775497
1010.5498593	11 8.7036655	12 8.9289235	13	
8.1749185	14 3.7815179	15 6.5897696	16	3.5520218
17				
0.4797585	18 -1.3755231	19 2.8867411		
Signal Line	0 0.0000000	1 0.7908928	2	1.4350954
3 2.6990553	4 4.3697977	5 4.7844607	6	
5.1413754	7 6.0070949	8 6.5940695	9	6.8107656
10 7.5585843	11 7.7876006	12 8.0158652	13	
8.0476758	14 7.1944442	15 7.0735093	16	6.3692118
17 4.9994178	18 3.7244296	19 3.5568919		

Python
Upper Bollinger Band:
NaN, NaN, NaN, NaN, NaN, NaN, 31.752242, 31.679116, 31.295640,
30.377123, 30.687927, 30.756538, 30.735017, 27.899515, 26.038009,
28.239415, 28.442307, 28.566102, 26.672172, 27.243837
Lower Bollinger Band:
NaN, NaN, NaN, NaN, NaN, NaN, 10.442698, 10.449312, 11.945889,
13.808783, 12.308626, 12.294762, 12.404659, 9.976811, 10.199543,
9.467071, 8.066317, 6.984086, 7.749454, 7.710677

6. Average True Range (ATR)

ATR is a technical analysis indicator used to measure market volatility. It
is often employed to assist traders in setting stop-loss levels, as well as to
determine the size of potential price movements.

```
# R
atr <- function(high_prices, low_prices, close_prices, n) {
```

```r
  atr_values <- ATR(High = high_prices, Low = low_prices, Close =
close_prices, n = n)
 return(atr_values)
}
```

```python
# Python
def atr(high_prices, low_prices, close_prices, n):
  true_range = pd.DataFrame({
    "TR1": high_prices - low_prices,
    "TR2": abs(high_prices - close_prices.shift()),
    "TR3": abs(low_prices - close_prices.shift())
  }).max(axis=1)
  atr_values = true_range.rolling(window=n).mean()
  return atr_values
```

Example

```r
# R Example
# Generating random data
set.seed(123)
high_prices <- runif(20, min = 1, max = 100)
low_prices <- runif(20, min = 1, max = 100)
close_prices <- runif(20, min = 1, max = 100)
n <- 14  # Period
atr <- function(high_prices, low_prices, close_prices, n) {
 true_range <- pmax(high_prices - low_prices, abs(high_prices -
lag(close_prices)), abs(low_prices - lag(close_prices)))
 atr_values <- zoo::rollmean(true_range, n, fill = NA)
 return(atr_values)
}
result <- atr(high_prices, low_prices, close_prices, n)
print(result)
```

```python
# Python Example
import pandas as pd
import numpy as np
# Generating random price data
np.random.seed(123)  # For reproducibility
high_prices = pd.Series(np.random.uniform(1, 100, 20))
low_prices = pd.Series(np.random.uniform(1, 100, 20))
close_prices = pd.Series(np.random.uniform(1, 100, 20))
n = 14  # Period
def atr(high_prices, low_prices, close_prices, n):
```

```
   true_range = pd.DataFrame({
     "TR1": high_prices - low_prices,
     "TR2": abs(high_prices - close_prices.shift()),
     "TR3": abs(low_prices - close_prices.shift())
   }).max(axis=1)
   atr_values = true_range.rolling(window=n).mean()
   return atr_values
result = atr(high_prices, low_prices, close_prices, n)
print(result)
```

Output summary
R
[1]   NA   NA   NA   NA   NA   NA 51.17120 49.68334
51.94290 54.80079 55.40769
[12] 53.91450 54.99751

R
13   44.037914 14   44.638671 15   45.260395 16   41.819392 17
43.110840 18   42.794337 19   41.594103

7. Stochastic Oscillator

This is a momentum indicator in technical analysis that compares a closing price to its price range over a specific period. It is used to identify overbought and oversold conditions in a market, helping traders anticipate potential price reversals.

```
# R
stochastic_oscillator <- function(high_prices, low_prices, close_prices,
n, k) {
  stoch <- stochasticOscillator(high_prices, low_prices, close_prices, n =
n, k = k)
  return(stoch)
}
```

```
# Python
def stochastic_oscillator(high_prices, low_prices, close_prices, n, k):
   lowest_low = low_prices.rolling(window=n).min()
   highest_high = high_prices.rolling(window=n).max()
   stoch_k = 100 * (close_prices - lowest_low) / (highest_high -
lowest_low)
   stoch_d = stoch_k.rolling(window=k).mean()
```

61

```
  return stoch_k, stoch_d
```

Example

```r
# R Example
set.seed(123)
high_prices <- runif(20, min = 1, max = 100)
low_prices <- runif(20, min = 1, max = 100)
close_prices <- runif(20, min = 1, max = 100)
n <- 14  # Period
k <- 3  # Smoothing period
stochastic_oscillator <- function(high_prices, low_prices, close_prices, n, k) {
  stoch_k <- numeric(length(high_prices))
  for (i in (n:length(high_prices))) {
    highest_high <- max(high_prices[(i - (n - 1)):i])
    lowest_low <- min(low_prices[(i - (n - 1)):i])
    stoch_k[i] <- 100 * (close_prices[i] - lowest_low) / (highest_high - lowest_low)
  }
  stoch_d <- SMA(stoch_k, n = k)
  return(list(stoch_k = stoch_k, stoch_d = stoch_d))
}
SMA <- function(x, n) {
  weights <- rep(1 / n, n)
  sma_values <- stats::filter(x, filter = weights, method = "convolution", sides = 1)
  return(sma_values)
}
result <- stochastic_oscillator(high_prices, low_prices, close_prices, n, k)
print(result)
```

```python
# Python Example
import pandas as pd
import numpy as np
# Generating random price data
np.random.seed(123)  # For reproducibility
high_prices = pd.Series(np.random.uniform(1, 100, 20))
low_prices = pd.Series(np.random.uniform(1, 100, 20))
close_prices = pd.Series(np.random.uniform(1, 100, 20))
n = 14  # Period
```

```
k = 3  # Smoothing period
def stochastic_oscillator(high_prices, low_prices, close_prices, n, k):
    lowest_low = low_prices.rolling(window=n).min()
    highest_high = high_prices.rolling(window=n).max()
    stoch_k = 100 * (close_prices - lowest_low) / (highest_high - lowest_low)
    stoch_d = stoch_k.rolling(window=k).mean()
    return stoch_k, stoch_d
stoch_k, stoch_d = stochastic_oscillator(high_prices, low_prices, close_prices, n, k)
print("Stochastic K:")
print(stoch_k)
print("\nStochastic D:")
print(stoch_d)
```

Output summary

R
$stoch_k [11]   0.000000   0.000000   0.000000 -3.113965 57.533039
19.514468 11.040098 78.167648 93.371950 37.528611
$stoch_d [11]   0.000000   0.000000   0.000000 -1.037988 18.139691
24.644514 29.362535 36.240738 60.859899 69.689403

Python
Stochastic K: 50.971513, 28.206412, 23.857946, 36.562638, 66.301658,
88.149861, 47.072868
Stochastic D:34.345290, 29.542332, 42.240748, 63.671386, 67.174796

8. Moving Average Convergence Divergence Histogram

MACD Histogram is a visual representation of the difference between the
MACD line and the Signal line. The MACD Histogram is used in
technical analysis to identify potential changes in the strength and
direction of a trend.

```
# R
macd_histogram <- function(price_data, n_fast, n_slow, n_signal) {
  macd_values <- MACD(price_data, nFast = n_fast, nSlow = n_slow,
nSig = n_signal)
  histogram <- macd_values$macd - macd_values$signal
  return(histogram)
}
```

```python
# Python
def macd_histogram(price_data, n_fast, n_slow, n_signal):
    ema_fast = price_data.ewm(span=n_fast, adjust=False).mean()
    ema_slow = price_data.ewm(span=n_slow, adjust=False).mean()
    macd_line = ema_fast - ema_slow
    signal_line = macd_line.ewm(span=n_signal, adjust=False).mean()
    histogram = macd_line - signal_line
    return histogram
```

Example

```r
# R Example
# Generating random price data
set.seed(123) # For reproducibility
price_data <- runif(40, min = 1, max = 100)

n_fast <- 12
n_slow <- 26
n_signal <- 9

macd_histogram <- function(price_data, n_fast, n_slow, n_signal) {
 ema_fast <- EMA(price_data, n_fast)
 ema_slow <- EMA(price_data, n_slow)
 macd_line <- ema_fast - ema_slow
 signal_line <- SMA(macd_line, n_signal)
 histogram <- macd_line - signal_line
 return(histogram)
}
EMA <- function(x, n) {
 weights <- rep(1/n, n)
 ema_values <- stats::filter(x, filter = weights, method = "recursive")
 return(ema_values)
}

SMA <- function(x, n) {
 sma_values <- stats::filter(x, filter = rep(1, n)/n, method = "convolution",
sides = 1)
 return(sma_values)
}
result <- macd_histogram(price_data, n_fast, n_slow, n_signal)
print(result)
```

```python
# Python Example
import pandas as pd
import numpy as np
# Generating random price data
np.random.seed(123)  # For reproducibility
price_data = pd.Series(np.random.uniform(1, 100, 40))
n_fast = 12
n_slow = 26
n_signal = 9
def macd_histogram(price_data, n_fast, n_slow, n_signal):
    ema_fast = price_data.ewm(span=n_fast, adjust=False).mean()
    ema_slow = price_data.ewm(span=n_slow, adjust=False).mean()
    macd_line = ema_fast - ema_slow
    signal_line = macd_line.ewm(span=n_signal, adjust=False).mean()
    histogram = macd_line - signal_line
    return histogram
result = macd_histogram(price_data, n_fast, n_slow, n_signal)
print(result)
```

Output

R
Time Series:
Start = 1
End = 40
Frequency = 1
 [1]   NA   NA   NA   NA   NA   NA   NA   NA 18.46976
20.34007 21.87433
[12] 25.66920 27.59756 28.59307 25.83969 23.79937 21.56967 16.53293
17.31643 16.02236 15.00215 16.40322
[23] 17.88593 15.19586 17.20078 15.90098 14.92819 18.06387 17.16744
18.40146 22.54941 27.84767 24.76957
[34] 23.15755 24.20764 21.03271 17.17412 18.23441 15.13652 14.86842

Python
0   0.000000   1   -2.592443   2   -4.450105   3   -3.315176
       4   -1.344040   5   -1.883846   6   1.430786   7
1.591333   8   0.344401   9   -0.993039   10   -2.062907
      11   -0.157164   12   0.759049   13   -3.457999   14   -
2.790367   15   -0.031253   16   -1.763242   17   -2.750189
      18   0.917855   19   0.339513   20   1.816125   21
4.059109   22   4.507460   23   3.870130   24   3.997508

65

25	1.360534	26	-0.104702	27	-1.847397	28	-
2.411312		29	-0.484043	30	2.630641	31	-1.649387
32	-0.931457	33	0.000756	34	0.192796	35	-
0.378417		36	0.041124	37	3.289469	38	5.503118
39	3.824311						

9. Commodity Channel Index (CCI)

The Commodity Channel Index (CCI) is a momentum-based technical indicator used in financial markets to assess the strength of a trend and identify potential reversal points.

```
# R
cci <- function(high_prices, low_prices, close_prices, n) {
 cci_values <- CCI(high_prices, low_prices, close_prices, n = n)
 return(cci_values)
}
```

```
# Python
def cci(high_prices, low_prices, close_prices, n):
    tp = (high_prices + low_prices + close_prices) / 3
    moving_average = tp.rolling(window=n).mean()
    mean_deviation          =          (tp          -
moving_average).abs().rolling(window=n).mean()
    cci_values = (tp - moving_average) / (0.015 * mean_deviation)
    return cci_values
```

Example

```
# R Example
high_prices <- c(50.22, 51.88, 53.53, 55.13, 54.33, 53.67, 53.64, 52.44,
52.98, 53.38)
low_prices <- c(48.98, 50.19, 51.09, 52.87, 52.35, 52.24, 52.08, 51.53,
51.55, 52.46)
close_prices <- c(49.74, 51.50, 52.77, 54.08, 53.87, 52.40, 52.26, 51.84,
52.02, 53.26)
n <- 5  # Period
cci <- function(high_prices, low_prices, close_prices, n) {
 tp <- (high_prices + low_prices + close_prices) / 3
 moving_average <- SMA(tp, n = n)
 mean_deviation <- SMA(abs(tp - moving_average), n = n)
 cci_values <- (tp - moving_average) / (0.015 * mean_deviation)
```

```r
  return(cci_values)
}
SMA <- function(x, n) {
  sma_values <- stats::filter(x, filter = rep(1/n, n), method =
"convolution", sides = 1)
  return(sma_values)
}
result <- cci(high_prices, low_prices, close_prices, n)
print(result)
```

```python
# Python Example
import pandas as pd
import numpy as np
# Generating random price data
np.random.seed(123)  # For reproducibility
high_prices = pd.Series(np.random.uniform(1, 100, 40))
low_prices = pd.Series(np.random.uniform(1, 100, 40))
close_prices = pd.Series(np.random.uniform(1, 100, 40))
n = 20  # Period
def cci(high_prices, low_prices, close_prices, n):
    tp = (high_prices + low_prices + close_prices) / 3
    moving_average = tp.rolling(window=n).mean()
    mean_deviation              =              (tp              -
moving_average).abs().rolling(window=n).mean()
    cci_values = (tp - moving_average) / (0.015 * mean_deviation)
    return cci_values
result = cci(high_prices, low_prices, close_prices, n)
print(result)
```

Outputs
R
-43.77927 70.50582
Python
38   -72.419157 39   132.385918

10. Fibonacci Retracement Levels

Fibonacci retracement levels are horizontal lines on a price chart that indicate potential levels of support or resistance based on key Fibonacci levels before the price continues in the original direction. These levels are based on the Fibonacci sequence, a mathematical concept where each number is the sum of the two preceding ones.

```R
#R Example:
# Function to calculate Fibonacci retracement levels
calculate_fibonacci_levels <- function(start_price, end_price) {
  retracement_levels <- c(0, 0.236, 0.382, 0.5, 0.618, 0.786, 1)
  retracement_prices <- start_price + retracement_levels * (end_price -
start_price)
  return(retracement_prices)
}
# Example usage
start_price <- 100  # Replace with your actual start price
end_price <- 150    # Replace with your actual end price
fibonacci_levels <- calculate_fibonacci_levels(start_price, end_price)
print(fibonacci_levels)
```

```python
# Python Example:
def calculate_fibonacci_levels(start_price, end_price):
    retracement_levels = [0, 0.236, 0.382, 0.5, 0.618, 0.786, 1]
    retracement_prices = [start_price + level * (end_price - start_price) for
level in retracement_levels]
    return retracement_prices
# Example usage
start_price = 100  # Replace with your actual start price
end_price = 150    # Replace with your actual end price
fibonacci_levels = calculate_fibonacci_levels(start_price, end_price)
print(fibonacci_levels)
```

Output
R
[1] 100.0 111.8 119.1 125.0 130.9 139.3 150.0
Python
[100, 111.8, 119.1, 125.0, 130.9, 139.3, 150]

11. Moving Average Convergence Divergence Signal Cross

The MACD Signal Cross is often used in conjunction with other technical indicators and analysis techniques to confirm signals and avoid false signals.

```r
# R
macd_signal_cross <- function(price_data, n_fast, n_slow, n_signal) {
 macd_values <- MACD(price_data, nFast = n_fast, nSlow = n_slow,
nSig = n_signal)
 signal_cross = ifelse(macd_values$macd > macd_values$signal, 1,
             ifelse(macd_values$macd < macd_values$signal, -1, 0))
 return(signal_cross)
}
```

```python
# Python
def macd_signal_cross(price_data, n_fast, n_slow, n_signal):
   ema_fast = price_data.ewm(span=n_fast, adjust=False).mean()
   ema_slow = price_data.ewm(span=n_slow, adjust=False).mean()
   macd_line = ema_fast - ema_slow
   signal_line = macd_line.ewm(span=n_signal, adjust=False).mean()
   signal_cross    =    np.where(macd_line    >    signal_line,   1,
np.where(macd_line < signal_line, -1, 0))
   return signal_cross
```

Example

```r
# R Example
# Generating random price data
set.seed(123) # For reproducibility
price_data <- runif(40, min = 1, max = 100)
n_fast <- 12
n_slow <- 26
n_signal <- 9
macd_signal_cross <- function(price_data, n_fast, n_slow, n_signal) {
 macd_values <- MACD(price_data, nFast = n_fast, nSlow = n_slow,
nSig = n_signal)
 signal_cross <- ifelse(macd_values$macd > macd_values$signal, 1,
             ifelse(macd_values$macd < macd_values$signal, -1, 0))
 return(signal_cross)
}
# Define a simple MACD function for demonstration purposes
MACD <- function(price_data, nFast, nSlow, nSig) {
 ema_fast <- EMA(price_data, n = nFast)
 ema_slow <- EMA(price_data, n = nSlow)
 macd_line <- ema_fast - ema_slow
 signal_line <- SMA(macd_line, n = nSig)
 macd_values <- data.frame(macd = macd_line, signal = signal_line)
```

```r
  return(macd_values)
}
EMA <- function(price_data, n) {
 ema_values <- runMean(price_data, n)
 return(ema_values)
}
SMA <- function(price_data, n) {
 sma_values <- runMean(price_data, n)
 return(sma_values)
}
result <- macd_signal_cross(price_data, n_fast, n_slow, n_signal)
print(result)
```

```python
# Python Example
import pandas as pd
import numpy as np
# Generating random price data
np.random.seed(456)  # For reproducibility
price_data = pd.Series(np.random.uniform(50, 150, 50))
n_fast = 10
n_slow = 20
n_signal = 5
def macd_signal_cross(price_data, n_fast, n_slow, n_signal):
   ema_fast = price_data.ewm(span=n_fast, adjust=False).mean()
   ema_slow = price_data.ewm(span=n_slow, adjust=False).mean()
   macd_line = ema_fast - ema_slow
   signal_line = macd_line.ewm(span=n_signal, adjust=False).mean()
   signal_cross    =    np.where(macd_line   >   signal_line,   1,
np.where(macd_line < signal_line, -1, 0))
   return signal_cross
result = macd_signal_cross(price_data, n_fast, n_slow, n_signal)
print(result)
```

Output
R
[36] 1 -1 1
Python
[0 -1 1...]

12. MACD Histogram Cross

Histogram Cross refers to the event when the histogram of the MACD indicator crosses above or below the zero line on a price chart.

```r
# R
macd_histogram_cross <- function(price_data, n_fast, n_slow, n_signal)
{
  macd_values <- MACD(price_data, nFast = n_fast, nSlow = n_slow,
nSig = n_signal)
  histogram = macd_values$macd - macd_values$signal
  histogram_cross = ifelse(histogram > 0, 1, ifelse(histogram < 0, -1, 0))
  return(histogram_cross)
}
```

```python
# Python
def macd_histogram_cross(price_data, n_fast, n_slow, n_signal):
    ema_fast = price_data.ewm(span=n_fast, adjust=False).mean()
    ema_slow = price_data.ewm(span=n_slow, adjust=False).mean()
    macd_line = ema_fast - ema_slow
    signal_line = macd_line.ewm(span=n_signal, adjust=False).mean()
    histogram = macd_line - signal_line
    histogram_cross = np.where(histogram > 0, 1, np.where(histogram < 0,
-1, 0))
    return histogram_cross
```

Example
```r
# R Example
set.seed(789)  # For reproducibility
price_data <- runif(50, min = 100, max = 200)
n_fast <- 10
n_slow <- 20
n_signal <- 5
macd_histogram_cross <- function(price_data, n_fast, n_slow, n_signal)
{
  macd_values <- MACD(price_data, nFast = n_fast, nSlow = n_slow,
nSig = n_signal)
  histogram <- macd_values$macd - macd_values$signal
  histogram_cross <- ifelse(histogram > 0, 1, ifelse(histogram < 0, -1, 0))
  return(histogram_cross)
}
```

```
# Define a simple MACD function for demonstration purposes
MACD <- function(price_data, nFast, nSlow, nSig) {
  ema_fast <- EMA(price_data, n = nFast)
  ema_slow <- EMA(price_data, n = nSlow)
  macd_line <- ema_fast - ema_slow
  signal_line <- SMA(macd_line, n = nSig)
  macd_values <- data.frame(macd = macd_line, signal = signal_line)
  return(macd_values)
}
EMA <- function(price_data, n) {
  ema_values <- runMean(price_data, n)
  return(ema_values)
}
SMA <- function(price_data, n) {
  sma_values <- runMean(price_data, n)
  return(sma_values)
}
result <- macd_histogram_cross(price_data, n_fast, n_slow, n_signal)
print(result)


# Python Example
import pandas as pd
import numpy as np
# Generating random price data
np.random.seed(789)  # For reproducibility
price_data = pd.Series(np.random.uniform(100, 200, 50))
n_fast = 10
n_slow = 20
n_signal = 5
def macd_histogram_cross(price_data, n_fast, n_slow, n_signal):
    ema_fast = price_data.ewm(span=n_fast, adjust=False).mean()
    ema_slow = price_data.ewm(span=n_slow, adjust=False).mean()
    macd_line = ema_fast - ema_slow
    signal_line = macd_line.ewm(span=n_signal, adjust=False).mean()
    histogram = macd_line - signal_line
    histogram_cross = np.where(histogram > 0, 1, np.where(histogram < 0,
-1, 0))
    return histogram_cross
result = macd_histogram_cross(price_data, n_fast, n_slow, n_signal)
print(result)
```

Output

R
[36] -1 -1...
Phyton
[0 -1 1...

13. Moving Average Golden Cross and Death Cross

The Moving Average Golden Cross and Death Cross are significant events in technical analysis, particularly when analyzing the relationship between short-term and long-term moving averages. The 50-day and 200-day SMAs are common choices, but other combinations, such as 20-day and 50-day can also be used based on the trader's strategy.

```
# R
moving_average_cross <- function(price_data, n_short, n_long) {
  short_ma = SMA(price_data, n = n_short)
  long_ma = SMA(price_data, n = n_long)
  cross = ifelse(short_ma > long_ma, 1, ifelse(short_ma < long_ma, -1, 0))
  return(cross)
}
# Python
def moving_average_cross(price_data, n_short, n_long):
  short_ma = price_data.rolling(window=n_short).mean()
  long_ma = price_data.rolling(window=n_long).mean()
  cross = np.where(short_ma > long_ma, 1, np.where(short_ma < long_ma, -1, 0))
  return cross
```

Example

```
# R Example
set.seed(123)  # For reproducibility
price_data <- runif(50, min = 50, max = 150)
n_short <- 5
n_long <- 20
moving_average_cross <- function(price_data, n_short, n_long) {
  short_ma <- SMA(price_data, n = n_short)
  long_ma <- SMA(price_data, n = n_long)
  cross <- ifelse(short_ma > long_ma, 1, ifelse(short_ma < long_ma, -1,
0))
```

73

```r
  return(cross)
}
SMA <- function(x, n) {
  sma_values <- stats::filter(x, filter = rep(1/n, n), method = "convolution",
sides = 1)
  return(sma_values)
}
result <- moving_average_cross(price_data, n_short, n_long)
print(result)
```

```python
# Python Example
import pandas as pd
import numpy as np
# Generating random price data
np.random.seed(123)  # For reproducibility
price_data = pd.Series(np.random.uniform(50, 150, 50))
n_short = 5
n_long = 20
def moving_average_cross(price_data, n_short, n_long):
    short_ma = price_data.rolling(window=n_short).mean()
    long_ma = price_data.rolling(window=n_long).mean()
    cross = np.where(short_ma > long_ma, 1, np.where(short_ma <
long_ma, -1, 0))
    return cross
result = moving_average_cross(price_data, n_short, n_long)
print(result)
```

Output

R [36] -1 -1…] Phyton [0 0 …]

14. RSI and Oversold Levels

The Relative Strength Index (RSI) is a momentum oscillator that measures the speed and change of price movements. It ranges from 0 to 100 and is typically used to identify overbought or oversold conditions in a market.

```r
# R
rsi_overbought_oversold <- function(rsi_values, overbought_level,
oversold_level) {
  overbought_oversold = ifelse(rsi_values > overbought_level, -1,
ifelse(rsi_values < oversold_level, 1, 0))
```

```
  return(overbought_oversold)
}

# Python
def rsi_overbought_oversold(rsi_values, overbought_level,
oversold_level):
   overbought_oversold = np.where(rsi_values > overbought_level, -1,
np.where(rsi_values < oversold_level, 1, 0))
   return overbought_oversold
```

Example

```
# R Example
set.seed(123)  # For reproducibility
rsi_values <- runif(50, min = 30, max = 70)
overbought_level <- 70
oversold_level <- 30
rsi_overbought_oversold <- function(rsi_values, overbought_level,
oversold_level) {
  overbought_oversold <- ifelse(rsi_values > overbought_level, -1,
ifelse(rsi_values < oversold_level, 1, 0))
  return(overbought_oversold)
}
result <- rsi_overbought_oversold(rsi_values, overbought_level,
oversold_level)
print(result)

# Python Example
import numpy as np
# Generating random RSI values
np.random.seed(123)  # For reproducibility
rsi_values = np.random.uniform(30, 70, 50)
overbought_level = 70
oversold_level = 30
def      rsi_overbought_oversold(rsi_values,      overbought_level,
oversold_level):
   overbought_oversold = np.where(rsi_values > overbought_level, -1,
np.where(rsi_values < oversold_level, 1, 0))
   return overbought_oversold
result    =    rsi_overbought_oversold(rsi_values,    overbought_level,
oversold_level)
print(result)
```

Output
R
[1] 0 0 0...]
Phyton
[0 0 0...]

15. MACD Zero Line Cross

Example for APPL stock from 2022 to 2023

```R
# R
# Function to calculate MACD and identify zero line cross
macd_zero_cross <- function(price_data, short_window, long_window,
signal_window) {
  # Calculate short-term and long-term EMAs
  short_ema <- EMA(price_data, n = short_window)
  long_ema <- EMA(price_data, n = long_window)
  # Calculate MACD line
  macd_line <- short_ema - long_ema
  # Calculate signal line
  signal_line <- EMA(macd_line, n = signal_window)
  # Identify zero line cross
  zero_cross <- ifelse(macd_line > 0 & macd_line > signal_line, "Buy",
              ifelse(macd_line < 0 & macd_line < signal_line, "Sell",
"No Signal"))
  # Combine results into a data frame
  result_df <- data.frame(Date = index(price_data),
                Price = as.numeric(price_data),
                MACD = macd_line,
                Signal = signal_line,
                ZeroCross = zero_cross)
  return(result_df)
}
# Example usage
library(quantmod)

# Download historical price data (replace 'AAPL' with your stock
symbol)
getSymbols("AAPL", src = "yahoo", from = "2022-01-01", to =
Sys.Date())
price_data <- Cl(AAPL)
```

```r
# Set parameters
short_window <- 12
long_window <- 26
signal_window <- 9
# Calculate MACD and identify zero line cross
macd_result <- macd_zero_cross(price_data, short_window,
long_window, signal_window)
# Print the result
print(macd_result)
```

```python
#Python
import pandas as pd
import ta
def macd_zero_cross(data, short_window, long_window,
signal_window):
    # Calculate the short-term EMA
    data['short_ema'] = ta.trend.ema_indicator(data['Close'],
window=short_window)
    # Calculate the long-term EMA
    data['long_ema'] = ta.trend.ema_indicator(data['Close'],
window=long_window)
    # Calculate MACD
    data['macd'] = data['short_ema'] - data['long_ema']
    # Calculate the signal line
    data['signal_line'] = ta.trend.ema_indicator(data['macd'],
window=signal_window)
    # Find where the MACD crosses above or below the signal line
    data['signal'] = 0
    data.loc[data['macd'] > data['signal_line'], 'signal'] = 1
    data.loc[data['macd'] < data['signal_line'], 'signal'] = -1
    # Find where the zero line is crossed
    data['zero_cross'] = 0
    data.loc[data['macd'] > 0, 'zero_cross'] = 1
    data.loc[data['macd'] < 0, 'zero_cross'] = -1
    return data
```

```python
# Example usage
# Assuming you have a DataFrame 'price_data' with a 'Close' column
# Adjust the parameters accordingly
short_window = 12
long_window = 26
signal_window = 9
```

```
price_data = pd.DataFrame({'Close': [82.74, 82.39, 83.03, 82.12, 81.89]})
result = macd_zero_cross(price_data, short_window, long_window,
signal_window)
print(result)
```

Output
R one line summary

Date		Price	MACD	Signal	ZeroCross
2022-03-28	2022-03-28	175.60	0.790961143	-2.673348777	Buy

Python line summary

	Close	short_ema	long_ema	macd	signal_line	signal	zero_cross
0	82.74	NaN	NaN	NaN	NaN	0	0

16. MACD Signal Line Cross

MACD Signal Line Cross to identify potential entry or exit points in the market. The crossover events are considered significant because they indicate changes in the trend momentum, potentially signaling the beginning of an uptrend or a downtrend.

R

```
# Install and load required packages
install.packages("quantmod")
library(quantmod)
# Function to calculate MACD Signal Line Cross
macd_signal_cross <- function(ticker, short_window, long_window,
signal_window) {
  # Download stock data
  getSymbols(ticker, src = "yahoo", from = "2022-01-01", to =
Sys.Date())
# Extract closing prices
  price_data <- Cl(get(ticker))
 # Calculate MACD
  macd_data <- MACD(price_data, nFast = short_window, nSlow =
long_window, nSig = signal_window)
# Create a data frame with relevant columns
  result <- data.frame(Date = index(macd_data), coredata(macd_data))
# Find where the MACD crosses above or below the signal line
  result$signal_cross <- ifelse(result$macd > result$signal, 1,
ifelse(result$macd < result$signal, -1, 0))
  return(result)
```

```
}
# Example usage
# Adjust the parameters accordingly
short_window <- 12
long_window <- 26
signal_window <- 9
# Replace 'AAPL' with your desired stock symbol
result <- macd_signal_cross("AAPL", short_window, long_window,
signal_window)
print(result)

# Python

import pandas as pd
import ta
# Function to calculate MACD Signal Line Cross
def macd_signal_cross(data, short_window, long_window,
signal_window):
    # Calculate MACD
    data['macd'] = ta.trend.MACD(data['Close'],
window_slow=long_window, window_fast=short_window,
window_sign=signal_window).macd()
    # Calculate Signal Line
    data['signal_line'] = ta.trend.MACD(data['Close'],
window_slow=long_window, window_fast=short_window,
window_sign=signal_window).macd_signal()
    # Find where the MACD crosses above or below the signal line
    data['signal_cross'] = 0
    data.loc[data['macd'] > data['signal_line'], 'signal_cross'] = 1
    data.loc[data['macd'] < data['signal_line'], 'signal_cross'] = -1
    return data
# Example usage
# Assuming you have a DataFrame 'price_data' with a 'Close' column
# Adjust the parameters accordingly
short_window = 5  # Adjusted the short_window to be within the valid
range
long_window = 12
signal_window = 9
price_data = pd.DataFrame({'Close': [82.74, 82.39, 83.03, 82.12, 81.89]})
result = macd_signal_cross(price_data, short_window, long_window,
signal_window)
print(result)
```

	Date	macd	signal	signal_cross
250	2022-12-29	-3.232034248	-2.444766401	-1

Python
Close macd signal_line signal_cross
0 82.74 NaN NaN 0

17. MACD Histogram Peak/Trough

The difference between the MACD line and the Signal line yields the MACD Histogram, which shows the momentum and strength of a trend graphically. Because they might shed light on a trend's strength and direction, traders frequently pay attention to the peaks and troughs on the MACD Histogram.

```r
# R
macd_histogram_peak_trough <- function(price_data, n_fast, n_slow, n_signal) {
  macd_values <- MACD(price_data, nFast = n_fast, nSlow = n_slow, nSig = n_signal)
  histogram = macd_values$macd - macd_values$signal
  peak_trough = ifelse(histogram > 0, -1, ifelse(histogram < 0, 1, 0))
  return(peak_trough)
}
```

```python
# Python
def macd_histogram_peak_trough(price_data, n_fast, n_slow, n_signal):
    ema_fast = price_data.ewm(span=n_fast, adjust=False).mean()
    ema_slow = price_data.ewm(span=n_slow, adjust=False).mean()
    macd_line = ema_fast - ema_slow
    signal_line = macd_line.ewm(span=n_signal, adjust=False).mean()
    histogram = macd_line - signal_line
    peak_trough = np.where(histogram > 0, -1, np.where(histogram < 0, 1, 0))
    return peak_trough
```

Output
R
[36] -1 -1 -1...
Phyton [0 -1 -1 -1...

18. MACD Zero Line Reversal

When the MACD line crosses the zero line, it may indicate a probable reversal in the prevailing trend. This is known as the Moving Average Convergence Divergence (MACD) Zero Line Reversal. A crossing above or below the MACD histogram's zero line, which represents a crucial level, can point to changes in the velocity and direction of the trend.

```r
# R
macd_zero_line_reversal <- function(price_data, n_fast, n_slow,
n_signal) {
  macd_values <- MACD(price_data, nFast = n_fast, nSlow = n_slow,
nSig = n_signal)
  zero_line_reversal = ifelse(macd_values$macd > 0 &
macd_values$macd < macd_values$signal, 1,
               ifelse(macd_values$macd < 0 & macd_values$macd
> macd_values$signal, -1, 0))
  return(zero_line_reversal)
}
```

```python
# Python
def macd_zero_line_reversal(price_data, n_fast, n_slow, n_signal):
    ema_fast = price_data.ewm(span=n_fast, adjust=False).mean()
    ema_slow = price_data.ewm(span=n_slow, adjust=False).mean()
    macd_line = ema_fast - ema_slow
    signal_line = macd_line.ewm(span=n_signal, adjust=False).mean()
    zero_line_reversal = np.where((macd_line > 0) & (macd_line <
signal_line), 1,
               np.where((macd_line < 0) & (macd_line >
signal_line), -1, 0))
    return zero_line_reversal
```

```r
# R Example
set.seed(123)  # For reproducibility
price_data <- runif(50, min = 50, max = 150)
n_fast <- 12
n_slow <- 26
n_signal <- 9
macd_zero_line_reversal <- function(price_data, n_fast, n_slow,
n_signal) {
```

```r
  macd_values <- MACD(price_data, nFast = n_fast, nSlow = n_slow,
nSig = n_signal)
  zero_line_reversal <- ifelse(macd_values$macd > 0 &
macd_values$macd < macd_values$signal, 1,
                    ifelse(macd_values$macd < 0 & macd_values$macd
> macd_values$signal, -1, 0))
  return(zero_line_reversal)
}

# Define a simple MACD function for demonstration purposes
MACD <- function(price_data, nFast, nSlow, nSig) {
  ema_fast <- EMA(price_data, n = nFast)
  ema_slow <- EMA(price_data, n = nSlow)
  macd_line <- ema_fast - ema_slow
  signal_line <- SMA(macd_line, n = nSig)
  macd_values <- data.frame(macd = macd_line, signal = signal_line)
  return(macd_values)
}
EMA <- function(price_data, n) {
  ema_values <- runMean(price_data, n)
  return(ema_values)
}
SMA <- function(price_data, n) {
  sma_values <- runMean(price_data, n)
  return(sma_values)
}
result <- macd_zero_line_reversal(price_data, n_fast, n_slow, n_signal)
print(result)

# Python Example
import pandas as pd
import numpy as np
# Generating random price data
np.random.seed(123)  # For reproducibility
price_data = pd.Series(np.random.uniform(50, 150, 50))
n_fast = 12
n_slow = 26
n_signal = 9
def macd_zero_line_reversal(price_data, n_fast, n_slow, n_signal):
    ema_fast = price_data.ewm(span=n_fast, adjust=False).mean()
    ema_slow = price_data.ewm(span=n_slow, adjust=False).mean()
    macd_line = ema_fast - ema_slow
```

```
  signal_line = macd_line.ewm(span=n_signal, adjust=False).mean()
  zero_line_reversal = np.where((macd_line > 0) & (macd_line <
signal_line), 1,
                    np.where((macd_line < 0) & (macd_line >
signal_line), -1, 0))
  return zero_line_reversal
result = macd_zero_line_reversal(price_data, n_fast, n_slow, n_signal)
print(result)
```

Outputs
R
[36] 0 0 0...]
Phyton
[0 0 0...]

19. Moving Average Ribbon

Plotting many moving averages over various time periods on a price chart
is how the Moving Average Ribbon, a technical analysis tool, is created.
The outcome is a pattern that resembles a ribbon and gives a visual
depiction of the trend's direction and overall strength. Example for APPL
stock form 2022-01-01 to 2023-11-18.

```
# R
moving_average_ribbon  <-  function(price_data,  short_terms,
long_terms) {
  ribbon = sapply(short_terms, function(short) {
   sma(price_data, n = short)
  })
  ribbon = rbind(ribbon, sapply(long_terms, function(long) {
   sma(price_data, n = long)
  }))
  return(ribbon)
}
```

```
# Python
def moving_average_ribbon(price_data, short_terms, long_terms):
  ribbon = np.vstack([
    np.array([sma(price_data, n=short_term) for short_term in
short_terms]),
    np.array([sma(price_data, n=long_term) for long_term in
long_terms])
```

```
  ])
  return ribbon
```

Example

```r
# R Example
# Install and load required packages
install.packages("quantmod")
library(quantmod)
# Function to calculate Moving Average Ribbon
moving_average_ribbon <- function(ticker, short_windows) {
  # Download stock data
  getSymbols(ticker, src = "yahoo", from = "2022-01-01", to =
Sys.Date())
  # Extract closing prices
  price_data <- Cl(get(ticker))
  # Create an empty data frame to store results
  result <- data.frame(Date = index(price_data))
  # Calculate moving averages for each window size
  for (window in short_windows) {
    result[paste0("MA_", window)] <- SMA(price_data, n = window)
  }
  return(result)
}
# Example usage
# Adjust the parameters accordingly
short_windows <- c(5, 10, 20)
# Replace 'AAPL' with your desired stock symbol
result <- moving_average_ribbon("AAPL", short_windows)
print(result)
```

```python
# Python Example
import yfinance as yf
import pandas as pd
import matplotlib.pyplot as plt
# Function to calculate Moving Average Ribbon
def moving_average_ribbon(ticker, short_windows):
    # Download stock data
    stock_data = yf.download(ticker, start="2022-01-01", end="2023-01-
01")
    # Calculate moving averages for each window size
    result = pd.DataFrame({"Date": stock_data.index})
```

```
  for window in short_windows:
    result[f"MA_{window}"] =
stock_data['Close'].rolling(window=window).mean()
  return result
# Example usage
# Adjust the parameters accordingly
short_windows = [5, 10, 20]
# Replace 'AAPL' with your desired stock symbol
result = moving_average_ribbon("AAPL", short_windows)
print(result)
```

Output
R line 250
        Date   MA_5   MA_10   MA_20
250 2022-12-29 129.954 132.090 138.2740
Python line 250
        Date MA_5 MA_10 MA_20
250 2022-12-30 NaN   NaN   NaN

20. Candlestick Patterns (Hammer and Shooting Star)

Traders use technical analysis to forecast future price movements, and these patterns are created by the arrangement of candlesticks on a price chart. The Hammer and Shooting Star candlestick patterns are examples of how price changes in financial markets are represented visually.

```
# R
candlestick_patterns <- function(open_prices, high_prices, low_prices,
close_prices) {
  hammer = ifelse((close_prices < open_prices) &
          ((open_prices - low_prices) / (0.001 + high_prices -
low_prices) > 0.6) &
          ((close_prices - low_prices) / (0.001 + high_prices -
low_prices) > 0.6), 1, 0)
  shooting_star = ifelse((open_prices < close_prices) &
            ((close_prices - low_prices) / (0.001 + high_prices -
low_prices) > 0.6) &
            ((open_prices - low_prices) / (0.001 + high_prices -
low_prices) > 0.6), -1, 0)
  return(hammer, shooting_star)
}
```

```python
# Python
def candlestick_patterns(open_prices, high_prices, low_prices,
close_prices):
    hammer = np.where(
        (close_prices < open_prices) &
        ((open_prices - low_prices) / (0.001 + high_prices - low_prices) >
0.6) &
        ((close_prices - low_prices) / (0.001 + high_prices - low_prices) >
0.6),
        1, 0
    )
    shooting_star = np.where(
        (open_prices < close_prices) &
        ((close_prices - low_prices) / (0.001 + high_prices - low_prices) >
0.6) &
        ((open_prices - low_prices) / (0.001 + high_prices - low_prices) >
0.6),
        -1, 0
    )
    return hammer, shooting_star
}
```

Example

```r
R
candlestick_patterns <- function(open_prices, high_prices, low_prices,
close_prices) {
  hammer = ifelse((close_prices < open_prices) &
        ((open_prices - low_prices) / (0.001 + high_prices -
low_prices) > 0.6) &
        ((close_prices - low_prices) / (0.001 + high_prices -
low_prices) > 0.6), 1, 0)
  shooting_star = ifelse((open_prices < close_prices) &
            ((close_prices - low_prices) / (0.001 + high_prices -
low_prices) > 0.6) &
            ((open_prices - low_prices) / (0.001 + high_prices -
low_prices) > 0.6), -1, 0)
  return(list(hammer = hammer, shooting_star = shooting_star))
}
# Example
open_prices <- c(100, 110, 90, 95, 120)
high_prices <- c(105, 115, 95, 100, 125)
```

```r
low_prices <- c(95, 105, 85, 90, 115)
close_prices <- c(102, 108, 92, 97, 122)
result <- candlestick_patterns(open_prices, high_prices, low_prices,
close_prices)
print(result$hammer)
print(result$shooting_star)
```

Python Example
```python
import numpy as np
def    candlestick_patterns(open_prices,    high_prices,    low_prices,
close_prices):
  hammer = np.where(
    (close_prices < open_prices) &
    ((open_prices - low_prices) / (0.001 + high_prices - low_prices) >
0.6) &
    ((close_prices - low_prices) / (0.001 + high_prices - low_prices) >
0.6),
    1, 0
  )
  shooting_star = np.where(
    (open_prices < close_prices) &
    ((close_prices - low_prices) / (0.001 + high_prices - low_prices) >
0.6) &
    ((open_prices - low_prices) / (0.001 + high_prices - low_prices) >
0.6),
    -1, 0
  )
  return hammer, shooting_star
# Example
open_prices = np.array([100, 110, 90, 95, 120])
high_prices = np.array([105, 115, 95, 100, 125])
low_prices = np.array([95, 105, 85, 90, 115])
close_prices = np.array([102, 108, 92, 97, 122])
hammer_result, shooting_star_result = candlestick_patterns(open_prices,
high_prices, low_prices, close_prices)
print("Hammer:", hammer_result)
print("Shooting Star:", shooting_star_result)
```
Outputs
R > print(result$hammer) [1] 0 0 0 0 0 > print(result$shooting_star)
[1] 0 0 0 0 0
Phyton Hammer: [0 0 0 0 0] Shooting Star: [0 0 0 0 0]

CHAPTER 3

This chapter covers twenty commonly used code examples for portfolio management calculations in both R and Python:

1. Portfolio Returns

The total performance, gain, or loss of a portfolio a group of investments or assets owned by an individual or an organization referred to as portfolio return. To calculate portfolio returns, one must evaluate the changes in the total value of each individual holding in the portfolio over a certain time.

```r
# R
portfolio_returns <- function(weights, returns) {
 portfolio_return <- sum(weights * returns)
 return(portfolio_return)
}
```

```python
# Python
def portfolio_returns(weights, returns):
    portfolio_return = sum(weights * returns)
    return portfolio_return
```

Example

```r
# R
weights <- c(0.3, 0.4, 0.3)
returns <- c(0.1, 0.05, 0.12)
portfolio_returns <- function(weights, returns) {
 portfolio_return <- sum(weights * returns)
 return(portfolio_return)
}
result <- portfolio_returns(weights, returns)
print(result)
```

```python
# Python
import numpy as np
weights = np.array([0.3, 0.4, 0.3])
returns = np.array([0.1, 0.05, 0.12])
```

```python
def portfolio_returns(weights, returns):
    portfolio_return = np.sum(weights * returns)
    return portfolio_return
result = portfolio_returns(weights, returns)
print(result)
```

Output: 0.086

2. Portfolio Volatility

The level of variance in a portfolio's returns over a certain period is measured by portfolio volatility. Investors use it as a crucial statistic for risk assessment to comprehend possible price volatility or variations in the value of their investment portfolio.

```r
# R
portfolio_volatility <- function(weights, cov_matrix) {
  portfolio_variance <- t(weights) %*% cov_matrix %*% weights
  portfolio_volatility <- sqrt(portfolio_variance)
  return(portfolio_volatility)
}
```

```python
# Python
import numpy as np
def portfolio_volatility(weights, cov_matrix):
    portfolio_variance = np.dot(weights.T, np.dot(cov_matrix, weights))
    portfolio_volatility = np.sqrt(portfolio_variance)
    return portfolio_volatility
```

Example

```r
# R
weights <- c(0.3, 0.4, 0.3)
cov_matrix <- matrix(c(0.1, 0.05, 0.02, 0.05, 0.12, 0.08, 0.02, 0.08, 0.15),
nrow = 3, ncol = 3, byrow = TRUE)
portfolio_volatility <- function(weights, cov_matrix) {
  portfolio_variance <- t(weights) %*% cov_matrix %*% weights
  portfolio_volatility <- sqrt(portfolio_variance)
  return(portfolio_volatility)
}
result <- portfolio_volatility(weights, cov_matrix)
print(result)
```

```python
# Python
import numpy as np
weights = np.array([0.3, 0.4, 0.3])
cov_matrix = np.array([[0.1, 0.05, 0.02], [0.05, 0.12, 0.08], [0.02, 0.08, 0.15]])
def portfolio_volatility(weights, cov_matrix):
    portfolio_variance = np.dot(weights.T, np.dot(cov_matrix, weights))
    portfolio_volatility = np.sqrt(portfolio_variance)
    return portfolio_volatility
result = portfolio_volatility(weights, cov_matrix)
print(result)
```

Output: 0.2765863

3. Portfolio Sharpe Ratio

The Portfolio Sharpe Ratio is a metric that evaluates a portfolio's risk-adjusted performance by considering both return and volatility. This ratio assists investors in determining whether a portfolio's returns sufficiently offset the degree of risk assumed.

```r
# R
portfolio_sharpe_ratio <- function(weights, returns, risk_free_rate, cov_matrix) {
  portfolio_return <- sum(weights * returns)
  portfolio_volatility <- sqrt(t(weights) %*% cov_matrix %*% weights)
  sharpe_ratio <- (portfolio_return - risk_free_rate) / portfolio_volatility
  return(sharpe_ratio)
}
```

```python
# Python
def portfolio_sharpe_ratio(weights, returns, risk_free_rate, cov_matrix):
    portfolio_return = sum(weights * returns)
    portfolio_volatility = np.sqrt(np.dot(weights.T, np.dot(cov_matrix, weights)))
    sharpe_ratio = (portfolio_return - risk_free_rate) / portfolio_volatility
    return sharpe_ratio
```

Example

```R
# R
weights <- c(0.3, 0.4, 0.3)
returns <- c(0.1, 0.05, 0.12)
risk_free_rate <- 0.02
cov_matrix <- matrix(c(0.1, 0.05, 0.02, 0.05, 0.12, 0.08, 0.02, 0.08, 0.15),
nrow = 3, ncol = 3, byrow = TRUE)
portfolio_sharpe_ratio <- function(weights, returns, risk_free_rate,
cov_matrix) {
  portfolio_return <- sum(weights * returns)
  portfolio_volatility <- sqrt(t(weights) %*% cov_matrix %*% weights)
  sharpe_ratio <- (portfolio_return - risk_free_rate) / portfolio_volatility
  return(sharpe_ratio)
}
result <- portfolio_sharpe_ratio(weights, returns, risk_free_rate,
cov_matrix)
print(result)
```

```python
# Python
import numpy as np
weights = np.array([0.3, 0.4, 0.3])
returns = np.array([0.1, 0.05, 0.12])
risk_free_rate = 0.02
cov_matrix = np.array([[0.1, 0.05, 0.02], [0.05, 0.12, 0.08], [0.02, 0.08,
0.15]])
def portfolio_sharpe_ratio(weights, returns, risk_free_rate, cov_matrix):
    portfolio_return = np.sum(weights * returns)
    portfolio_volatility = np.sqrt(np.dot(weights.T, np.dot(cov_matrix,
weights)))
    sharpe_ratio = (portfolio_return - risk_free_rate) / portfolio_volatility
    return sharpe_ratio
result = portfolio_sharpe_ratio(weights, returns, risk_free_rate,
cov_matrix)
print(result)
```

Output 0.2386235

4. Minimum Variance Portfolio

A portfolio allocation known as the Minimum Variance Portfolio aims to reduce the total volatility or variance of returns. It is a fundamental idea in modern portfolio theory. Portfolios that offer the highest expected return for a given level of risk, or the lowest risk for a given level of expected return, can be created by investors.

```r
# R
minimum_variance_portfolio <- function(cov_matrix) {
 inv_cov_matrix <- solve(cov_matrix)
 ones <- rep(1, length(cov_matrix))
 min_variance_weights   <-   inv_cov_matrix   %*%   ones   /
sum(inv_cov_matrix %*% ones)
 return(min_variance_weights)
}
```

```python
# Python
def minimum_variance_portfolio(cov_matrix):
   inv_cov_matrix = np.linalg.inv(cov_matrix)
   ones = np.ones(len(cov_matrix))
   min_variance_weights   =   np.dot(inv_cov_matrix,   ones)   /
np.sum(np.dot(inv_cov_matrix, ones))
   return min_variance_weights
```

Example

```r
# R
cov_matrix <- matrix(c(0.1, 0.05, 0.02, 0.05, 0.12, 0.08, 0.02, 0.08, 0.15),
nrow = 3, ncol = 3, byrow = TRUE)
minimum_variance_portfolio <- function(cov_matrix) {
 inv_cov_matrix <- solve(cov_matrix)
 ones <- matrix(1, nrow = nrow(cov_matrix), ncol = 1)
 min_variance_weights   <-   inv_cov_matrix   %*%   ones   /
sum(inv_cov_matrix %*% ones)
 return(min_variance_weights)
}
result <- minimum_variance_portfolio(cov_matrix)
print(result)
```

```python
# Python
import numpy as np
cov_matrix = np.array([[0.1, 0.05, 0.02], [0.05, 0.12, 0.08], [0.02, 0.08,
0.15]])
def minimum_variance_portfolio(cov_matrix):
   inv_cov_matrix = np.linalg.inv(cov_matrix)
   ones = np.ones(len(cov_matrix))
```

```
    min_variance_weights    =    np.dot(inv_cov_matrix,    ones)    /
np.sum(np.dot(inv_cov_matrix, ones))
    return min_variance_weights
result = minimum_variance_portfolio(cov_matrix)
print(result)
```

Output
R
[1,] 0.5572519
[2,] 0.1297710
[3,] 0.3129771
Python
[0.55725191 0.12977099 0.3129771]

5. Capital Market Line (CML) Portfolio

In finance, the term "Capital Market Line" (CML) refers to a theoretical
line that, usually within the framework of the Capital Asset Pricing Model,
illustrates the connection between risk and return for a portfolio of riskier
assets (CAPM). From the risk-free rate to a location tangent to the
efficient frontier of risky assets, the CML is a straight line.

```
# R
cml_portfolio <- function(risk_free_rate, cml_slope, portfolio_volatility)
{
  cml_return = risk_free_rate + cml_slope * portfolio_volatility
  return(cml_return)
}
```

```
# Python
def cml_portfolio(risk_free_rate, cml_slope, portfolio_volatility):
    cml_return = risk_free_rate + cml_slope * portfolio_volatility
    return cml_return
```

Example

```
# R
risk_free_rate <- 0.02
cml_slope <- 0.05
portfolio_volatility <- 0.1
cml_portfolio <- function(risk_free_rate, cml_slope, portfolio_volatility)
{
```

```
  cml_return <- risk_free_rate + cml_slope * portfolio_volatility
  return(cml_return)
}
result <- cml_portfolio(risk_free_rate, cml_slope, portfolio_volatility)
print(result)

# Python
risk_free_rate = 0.02
cml_slope = 0.05
portfolio_volatility = 0.1
def cml_portfolio(risk_free_rate, cml_slope, portfolio_volatility):
    cml_return = risk_free_rate + cml_slope * portfolio_volatility
    return cml_return
result = cml_portfolio(risk_free_rate, cml_slope, portfolio_volatility)
print(result)
```

Output
0.025

6. Efficient Frontier

The Efficient Frontier is a key concept which represents the set of optimal portfolios that offer the maximum expected return for a given level of risk or the minimum risk for a given level of expected return. Efficient portfolios offer the optimal balance between return and risk as they are situated on the Efficient Frontier.

```
# R
efficient_frontier <- function(returns, cov_matrix, num_portfolios) {
  results <- matrix(NA, ncol = 3, nrow = num_portfolios)
  colnames(results) <- c("Return", "Volatility", "Sharpe Ratio")
  for (i in 1:num_portfolios) {
    weights <- runif(length(returns))
    weights <- weights / sum(weights)
    portfolio_return <- sum(weights * returns)
    portfolio_volatility <- sqrt(t(weights) %*% cov_matrix %*% weights)
    sharpe_ratio <- portfolio_return / portfolio_volatility
    results[i, ] <- c(portfolio_return, portfolio_volatility, sharpe_ratio)
  }
  return(results)
}
```

```python
# Python
def efficient_frontier(returns, cov_matrix, num_portfolios):
    results = np.zeros((num_portfolios, 3))
    for i in range(num_portfolios):
        weights = np.random.random(len(returns))
        weights /= np.sum(weights)
        portfolio_return = np.sum(weights * returns)
        portfolio_volatility = np.sqrt(np.dot(weights.T, np.dot(cov_matrix, weights)))
        sharpe_ratio = portfolio_return / portfolio_volatility
        results[i, :] = [portfolio_return, portfolio_volatility, sharpe_ratio]
    return results
```

Example

```r
# R
num_portfolios <- 5
returns <- c(0.1, 0.05, 0.12)
cov_matrix <- matrix(c(0.1, 0.05, 0.02, 0.05, 0.12, 0.08, 0.02, 0.08, 0.15),
nrow = 3, ncol = 3, byrow = TRUE)

efficient_frontier <- function(returns, cov_matrix, num_portfolios) {
  results <- matrix(NA, ncol = 3, nrow = num_portfolios)
  colnames(results) <- c("Return", "Volatility", "Sharpe Ratio")
  for (i in 1:num_portfolios) {
    weights <- runif(length(returns))
    weights <- weights / sum(weights)
    portfolio_return <- sum(weights * returns)
    portfolio_volatility <- sqrt(t(weights) %*% cov_matrix %*% weights)
    sharpe_ratio <- portfolio_return / portfolio_volatility
    results[i, ] <- c(portfolio_return, portfolio_volatility, sharpe_ratio)
  }
  return(results)
}
result <- efficient_frontier(returns, cov_matrix, num_portfolios)
print(result)
```

```python
# Python
import numpy as np
num_portfolios = 5
returns = np.array([0.1, 0.05, 0.12])
```

```
cov_matrix = np.array([[0.1, 0.05, 0.02], [0.05, 0.12, 0.08], [0.02, 0.08, 0.15]])
def efficient_frontier(returns, cov_matrix, num_portfolios):
    results = np.zeros((num_portfolios, 3))
    for i in range(num_portfolios):
        weights = np.random.random(len(returns))
        weights /= np.sum(weights)
        portfolio_return = np.sum(weights * returns)
        portfolio_volatility = np.sqrt(np.dot(weights.T, np.dot(cov_matrix, weights)))
        sharpe_ratio = portfolio_return / portfolio_volatility
        results[i, :] = [portfolio_return, portfolio_volatility, sharpe_ratio]
    return results
result = efficient_frontier(returns, cov_matrix, num_portfolios)
print(result)
```

Output

R

	Return	Volatility	Sharpe Ratio
[1,]	0.09523565	0.3291460	0.2893417
[2,]	0.07310845	0.3017558	0.2422768
[3,]	0.08887063	0.3145006	0.2825769
[4,]	0.07235681	0.2854732	0.2534627
[5,]	0.10174720	0.2897313	0.3511778

Python
```
[[0.08534956 0.27684869 0.30828954]
 [0.10634645 0.26873524 0.39572947]
 [0.08518059 0.27605724 0.30856133]
 [0.08485062 0.27646624 0.30691131]
 [0.09982499 0.2738654  0.36450386]]
```

7. Risk Parity Portfolio

An investment portfolio built with the intention of distributing risk evenly among various assets or asset classes is known as a risk parity portfolio. To balance each component's contribution to the portfolio's overall risk is the central principle of risk parity.

```
# R
risk_parity_portfolio <- function(cov_matrix) {
```

```
  inv_cov_matrix <- solve(cov_matrix)
  ones <- rep(1, length(cov_matrix))
  risk_contributions <- (inv_cov_matrix %*% ones) /
sum(inv_cov_matrix %*% ones)
  risk_parity_weights <- risk_contributions / sum(risk_contributions)
  return(risk_parity_weights)
}
```

```
# Python
def risk_parity_portfolio(cov_matrix):
  inv_cov_matrix = np.linalg.inv(cov_matrix)
  ones = np.ones(len(cov_matrix))
  risk_contributions = np.dot(inv_cov_matrix, ones) /
np.sum(np.dot(inv_cov_matrix, ones))
  risk_parity_weights = risk_contributions / np.sum(risk_contributions)
  return risk_parity_weights
```

Example

```
# R
cov_matrix <- matrix(c(0.1, 0.05, 0.02, 0.05, 0.12, 0.08, 0.02, 0.08, 0.15),
nrow = 3, ncol = 3, byrow = TRUE)
risk_parity_portfolio <- function(cov_matrix) {
  inv_cov_matrix <- solve(cov_matrix)
  ones <- matrix(1, nrow = nrow(cov_matrix), ncol = 1)  # Defining 'ones'
as a column matrix
  risk_contributions    <-    (inv_cov_matrix    %*%    ones)    /
sum(inv_cov_matrix %*% ones)
  risk_parity_weights <- risk_contributions / sum(risk_contributions)
  return(risk_parity_weights)
}
result <- risk_parity_portfolio(cov_matrix)
print(result)
```

```
# Python
import numpy as np
cov_matrix = np.array([[0.1, 0.05, 0.02], [0.05, 0.12, 0.08], [0.02, 0.08,
0.15]])
def risk_parity_portfolio(cov_matrix):
  inv_cov_matrix = np.linalg.inv(cov_matrix)
  ones = np.ones(len(cov_matrix))
```

```
risk_contributions       =       np.dot(inv_cov_matrix,       ones)       /
np.sum(np.dot(inv_cov_matrix, ones))
   risk_parity_weights = risk_contributions / np.sum(risk_contributions)
   return risk_parity_weights
result = risk_parity_portfolio(cov_matrix)
print(result)
```

Output
R
[1,] 0.5572519
[2,] 0.1297710
[3,] 0.3129771

Python
[0.55725191 0.12977099 0.3129771]

8. Maximum Drawdown

The highest peak-to-trough decrease or loss in the value of an investment or portfolio over a certain period is measured by a risk indicator called maximum drawdown, or MDD. It gives insight on the largest loss an investor would have sustained over a specific time frame for investments.

```
# R
max_drawdown <- function(returns) {
  cum_returns <- cumprod(1 + returns)
  peak <- cummax(cum_returns)
  drawdown <- (cum_returns - peak) / peak
  max_drawdown <- max(drawdown)
  return(max_drawdown)
}
```

```
# Python
def max_drawdown(returns):
   cum_returns = np.cumprod(1 + returns)
   peak = np.maximum.accumulate(cum_returns)
   drawdown = (cum_returns - peak) / peak
   max_drawdown = np.max(drawdown)
   return max_drawdown
```

Example

```r
# R
returns <- c(0.1, -0.05, 0.03, -0.02, 0.04)
max_drawdown <- function(returns) {
  cum_returns <- cumprod(1 + returns)
  peak <- cummax(cum_returns)
  drawdown <- (cum_returns - peak) / peak
  max_drawdown <- max(drawdown)
  return(max_drawdown)
}
result <- max_drawdown(returns)
print(result)
```

```python
# Python
import numpy as np
returns = np.array([0.1, -0.05, 0.03, -0.02, 0.04])
def max_drawdown(returns):
    cum_returns = np.cumprod(1 + returns)
    peak = np.maximum.accumulate(cum_returns)
    drawdown = (cum_returns - peak) / peak
    max_drawdown = np.max(drawdown)
    return max_drawdown
result = max_drawdown(returns)
print(result)
```

Output
R [1] 0 Python 0.0

9. Tracking Error

The standard deviation of the difference between the returns of an investment portfolio and the returns of a benchmark index is measured using a metric called tracking error. Investors and portfolio managers consider it as a critical statistic to evaluate how effectively a portfolio is following or imitating its benchmark.

```r
# R
tracking_error <- function(portfolio_returns, benchmark_returns) {
  excess_returns <- portfolio_returns - benchmark_returns
  tracking_error <- sd(excess_returns)
  return(tracking_error)
}
```

```python
# Python
def tracking_error(portfolio_returns, benchmark_returns):
    excess_returns = portfolio_returns - benchmark_returns
    tracking_error = np.std(excess_returns)
    return tracking_error
```

Example

```r
# R
portfolio_returns <- c(0.1, 0.05, 0.12, 0.08, 0.11)
benchmark_returns <- c(0.05, 0.03, 0.11, 0.07, 0.09)
tracking_error <- function(portfolio_returns, benchmark_returns) {
  excess_returns <- portfolio_returns - benchmark_returns
  tracking_error <- sd(excess_returns)
  return(tracking_error)
}
result <- tracking_error(portfolio_returns, benchmark_returns)
print(result)
```

```python
# Python
import numpy as np
portfolio_returns = np.array([0.1, 0.05, 0.12, 0.08, 0.11])
benchmark_returns = np.array([0.05, 0.03, 0.11, 0.07, 0.09])
def tracking_error(portfolio_returns, benchmark_returns):
    excess_returns = portfolio_returns - benchmark_returns
    tracking_error = np.std(excess_returns)
    return tracking_error
result = tracking_error(portfolio_returns, benchmark_returns)
print(result)
```

Output
0.01643168

10. Active Return

Excess Return, another name for Active Return, is a metric used to quantify the discrepancy between an investment portfolio's real return and the return of a selected benchmark index.

```r
# R
active_return <- function(portfolio_returns, benchmark_returns) {
  active_returns <- portfolio_returns - benchmark_returns
```

```
  return(active_returns)
}
```

```
# Python
def active_return(portfolio_returns, benchmark_returns):
    active_returns = portfolio_returns - benchmark_returns
    return active_returns
```

Example

```
# R
portfolio_returns <- c(0.1, 0.05, 0.12, 0.08, 0.11)
benchmark_returns <- c(0.05, 0.03, 0.11, 0.07, 0.09)
active_return <- function(portfolio_returns, benchmark_returns) {
  active_returns <- portfolio_returns - benchmark_returns
  return(active_returns)
}
result <- active_return(portfolio_returns, benchmark_returns)
print(result)
```

```
# Python
import numpy as np
portfolio_returns = np.array([0.1, 0.05, 0.12, 0.08, 0.11])
benchmark_returns = np.array([0.05, 0.03, 0.11, 0.07, 0.09])
def active_return(portfolio_returns, benchmark_returns):
    active_returns = portfolio_returns - benchmark_returns
    return active_returns
result = active_return(portfolio_returns, benchmark_returns)
print(result)
```

Output
R
[1] 0.05 0.02 0.01 0.01 0.02
Python
[0.05 0.02 0.01 0.01 0.02]

11. Information Ratio

The Information Ratio is a risk-adjusted performance indicator that
evaluates a fund manager's or investment portfolio's capacity to produce
excess returns above a benchmark while taking the amount of risk
assumed into account.

```r
# R
information_ratio <- function(active_returns, tracking_error) {
  information_ratio <- mean(active_returns) / tracking_error
  return(information_ratio)
}
```

```python
# Python
def information_ratio(active_returns, tracking_error):
    information_ratio = np.mean(active_returns) / tracking_error
    return information_ratio
```

Example

```r
# R
active_returns <- c(0.02, -0.01, 0.03, 0.01, -0.02)
tracking_error <- 0.015
information_ratio <- function(active_returns, tracking_error) {
  information_ratio <- mean(active_returns) / tracking_error
  return(information_ratio)
}
result <- information_ratio(active_returns, tracking_error)
print(result)
```

```python
# Python
import numpy as np
active_returns = np.array([0.02, -0.01, 0.03, 0.01, -0.02])
tracking_error = 0.015
def information_ratio(active_returns, tracking_error):
    information_ratio = np.mean(active_returns) / tracking_error
    return information_ratio
result = information_ratio(active_returns, tracking_error)
print(result)
```

Output
0.4

12. Treynor Ratio

A risk-adjusted performance measure called the Treynor Ratio assesses an investment portfolio's return in relation to beta, or unit of systematic risk.

It is a measurement of the extra return obtained for every unit of systematic risk assumed over the risk-free rate.

```r
# R
treynor_ratio <- function(portfolio_return, risk_free_rate, beta) {
  treynor_ratio <- (portfolio_return - risk_free_rate) / beta
  return(treynor_ratio)
}
```

```python
# Python
def treynor_ratio(portfolio_return, risk_free_rate, beta):
    treynor_ratio = (portfolio_return - risk_free_rate) / beta
    return treynor_ratio
```

Example

```r
# R
portfolio_return <- 0.08
risk_free_rate <- 0.03
beta <- 1.2
treynor_ratio <- function(portfolio_return, risk_free_rate, beta) {
  treynor_ratio <- (portfolio_return - risk_free_rate) / beta
  return(treynor_ratio)
}
result <- treynor_ratio(portfolio_return, risk_free_rate, beta)
print(result)
```

```python
# Python
portfolio_return = 0.08
risk_free_rate = 0.03
beta = 1.2
def treynor_ratio(portfolio_return, risk_free_rate, beta):
    treynor_ratio = (portfolio_return - risk_free_rate) / beta
    return treynor_ratio
result = treynor_ratio(portfolio_return, risk_free_rate, beta)
print(result)
```

Output
R
0.04166667
Python
0.04166666666666667

13. Sortino Ratio

A risk-adjusted performance measure called the Sortino Ratio assesses an investment portfolio's return in relation to its downside risk, paying particular attention to the volatility of negative returns.

```r
# R
sortino_ratio <- function(portfolio_return, risk_free_rate,
downside_deviation) {
  sortino_ratio <- (portfolio_return - risk_free_rate) / downside_deviation
  return(sortino_ratio)
}
```

```python
# Python
def sortino_ratio(portfolio_return, risk_free_rate, downside_deviation):
    sortino_ratio = (portfolio_return - risk_free_rate) / downside_deviation
    return sortino_ratio
```

Example

```r
# R
portfolio_return <- 0.08
risk_free_rate <- 0.03
downside_deviation <- 0.05
sortino_ratio       <-       function(portfolio_return,       risk_free_rate,
downside_deviation) {
  sortino_ratio <- (portfolio_return - risk_free_rate) / downside_deviation
  return(sortino_ratio)
}
result       <-       sortino_ratio(portfolio_return,       risk_free_rate,
downside_deviation)
print(result)
```

```python
# Python
portfolio_return = 0.08
risk_free_rate = 0.03
downside_deviation = 0.05
def sortino_ratio(portfolio_return, risk_free_rate, downside_deviation):
    sortino_ratio = (portfolio_return - risk_free_rate) / downside_deviation
    return sortino_ratio
result       =       sortino_ratio(portfolio_return,       risk_free_rate,
downside_deviation)
```

```
print(result)
```

Output
1.0

14. Conditional Value-at-Risk (CVaR)

Expected Shortfall (ES), another name for Conditional Value-at-Risk (CVaR), is a risk metric that evaluates the average value of losses over a given confidence threshold. In contrast to Value-at-Risk (VaR), which gives a maximum loss with a certain probability as a threshold value, CVaR averages the losses that are greater than this threshold.

```
# R
cvar <- function(returns, alpha) {
  cvar_value <- quantile(returns, probs = alpha)
  return(cvar_value)
}
```

```
# Python
def cvar(returns, alpha):
    cvar_value = np.percentile(returns, q=100 * alpha)
    return cvar_value
```

Example

```
# R
returns <- c(0.02, -0.01, 0.03, 0.01, -0.02)
alpha <- 0.05
cvar <- function(returns, alpha) {
  cvar_value <- quantile(returns, probs = alpha)
  return(cvar_value)
}
result <- cvar(returns, alpha)
print(result)
```

```
# Python
import numpy as np
returns = np.array([0.02, -0.01, 0.03, 0.01, -0.02])
alpha = 0.05
def cvar(returns, alpha):
    cvar_value = np.percentile(returns, q=100 * alpha)
```

```
    return cvar_value
result = cvar(returns, alpha)
print(result)
```

Output
R
  5%
-0.018
Python
-0.018000000000000002

15. Value-at-Risk (VaR)

A popular risk management statistic called Value-at-Risk measures the potential loss in an investment's or portfolio's value over a given period with a particular degree of confidence.

```
# R
var <- function(returns, alpha) {
 var_value <- quantile(returns, probs = alpha)
 return(var_value)
}
```

```
# Python
def var(returns, alpha):
    var_value = np.percentile(returns, q=100 * alpha)
    return var_value
```

Example

```
# R
returns <- c(0.03, 0.02, 0.05, -0.01, -0.02, 0.04, -0.03, 0.01, 0.02, -0.02)
alpha <- 0.1
var <- function(returns, alpha) {
 var_value <- quantile(returns, probs = alpha)
 return(var_value)
}
result <- var(returns, alpha)
print(result)
```

```
# Python
```

```
import numpy as np
returns = np.array([0.03, 0.02, 0.05, -0.01, -0.02, 0.04, -0.03, 0.01, 0.02, -0.02])
alpha = 0.1
def var(returns, alpha):
    var_value = np.percentile(returns, q=100 * alpha)
    return var_value
result = var(returns, alpha)
print(result)
```

Output
R
  10%
-0.021
Python
-0.021

16. Portfolio Beta

Portfolio beta, which is commonly abbreviated as beta, quantifies the degree of systematic risk or sensitivity of a portfolio's returns to variations in the returns of the general market. Investors may determine how much a portfolio's value is expected to fluctuate in reaction to market movements by using beta, a crucial indicator in finance and portfolio management.

```
# R
portfolio_beta <- function(weights, asset_betas) {
  portfolio_beta <- sum(weights * asset_betas)
  return(portfolio_beta)
}
```

```
# Python
def portfolio_beta(weights, asset_betas):
    portfolio_beta = np.sum(weights * asset_betas)
    return portfolio_beta
```

Example

```
# R
weights <- c(0.4, 0.3, 0.3)
asset_betas <- c(1.2, 0.8, 1.5)
```

```r
portfolio_beta <- function(weights, asset_betas) {
  portfolio_beta <- sum(weights * asset_betas)
  return(portfolio_beta)
}
result <- portfolio_beta(weights, asset_betas)
print(result)
```

```python
# Python
import numpy as np
weights = np.array([0.4, 0.3, 0.3])
asset_betas = np.array([1.2, 0.8, 1.5])
def portfolio_beta(weights, asset_betas):
    portfolio_beta = np.sum(weights * asset_betas)
    return portfolio_beta
result = portfolio_beta(weights, asset_betas)
print(result)
```

Output
1.17

17. Portfolio Alpha

Portfolio alpha, commonly known as just alpha, is a metric used to evaluate the risk-adjusted performance of a portfolio by comparing its returns to an expected return or benchmark. A fundamental idea in modern portfolio theory, alpha is used to assess an investment manager's ability to produce returns that are higher than anticipated given the amount of risk taken.

```r
# R
portfolio_alpha      <-      function(portfolio_return,      risk_free_rate,
portfolio_beta, benchmark_return) {
  portfolio_alpha <- portfolio_return - (risk_free_rate + portfolio_beta *
(benchmark_return - risk_free_rate))
  return(portfolio_alpha)
}
```

```python
# Python
def  portfolio_alpha(portfolio_return,  risk_free_rate,  portfolio_beta,
benchmark_return):
    portfolio_alpha = portfolio_return - (risk_free_rate + portfolio_beta *
(benchmark_return - risk_free_rate))
```

```
  return portfolio_alpha
```

Example

```r
# R
portfolio_return <- 0.1
risk_free_rate <- 0.05
portfolio_beta <- 1.2
benchmark_return <- 0.08
portfolio_alpha      <-      function(portfolio_return,      risk_free_rate,
portfolio_beta, benchmark_return) {
  portfolio_alpha <- portfolio_return - (risk_free_rate + portfolio_beta *
(benchmark_return - risk_free_rate))
  return(portfolio_alpha)
}
result <- portfolio_alpha(portfolio_return, risk_free_rate, portfolio_beta,
benchmark_return)
print(result)
```

```python
# Python
portfolio_return = 0.1
risk_free_rate = 0.05
portfolio_beta = 1.2
benchmark_return = 0.08
def  portfolio_alpha(portfolio_return,  risk_free_rate,  portfolio_beta,
benchmark_return):
    portfolio_alpha = portfolio_return - (risk_free_rate + portfolio_beta *
(benchmark_return - risk_free_rate))
    return portfolio_alpha
result = portfolio_alpha(portfolio_return, risk_free_rate, portfolio_beta,
benchmark_return)
print(result)
```

Output
R
[1] 0.014
Python
0.014000000000000012

18. Jensen's Alpha

A risk-adjusted performance statistic called Jensen's Alpha, or Jensen's Performance Index, is used in the financial industry to assess the excess return of an asset manager or investment portfolio in comparison to a benchmark.

```r
# R
jensens_alpha <- function(portfolio_return, risk_free_rate, portfolio_beta, benchmark_return) {
  jensens_alpha <- portfolio_return - (risk_free_rate + portfolio_beta * (benchmark_return - risk_free_rate))
  return(jensens_alpha)
}
```

```python
# Python
def jensens_alpha(portfolio_return, risk_free_rate, portfolio_beta, benchmark_return):
    jensens_alpha = portfolio_return - (risk_free_rate + portfolio_beta * (benchmark_return - risk_free_rate))
    return jensens_alpha
```

Example

```r
# R
portfolio_return <- 0.12
risk_free_rate <- 0.06
portfolio_beta <- 1.5
benchmark_return <- 0.1
jensens_alpha <- function(portfolio_return, risk_free_rate, portfolio_beta, benchmark_return) {
  jensens_alpha <- portfolio_return - (risk_free_rate + portfolio_beta * (benchmark_return - risk_free_rate))
  return(jensens_alpha)
}
result <- jensens_alpha(portfolio_return, risk_free_rate, portfolio_beta, benchmark_return)
print(result)
```

```python
# Python
portfolio_return = 0.12
risk_free_rate = 0.06
```

```
portfolio_beta = 1.5
benchmark_return = 0.1
def jensens_alpha(portfolio_return, risk_free_rate, portfolio_beta,
benchmark_return):
    jensens_alpha = portfolio_return - (risk_free_rate + portfolio_beta *
(benchmark_return - risk_free_rate))
    return jensens_alpha
result = jensens_alpha(portfolio_return, risk_free_rate, portfolio_beta,
benchmark_return)
print(result)
```

Output
R
[1] -1.387779e-17
Python
-1.3877787807814457e-17

19. Portfolio Turnover

A metric known as portfolio turnover quantifies how frequently the assets
in an investment portfolio are purchased and sold over a given time frame.
It indicates the degree to which the portfolio's composition varies over
time and is given as a percentage.

```
# R
portfolio_turnover <- function(weights_t1, weights_t2) {
  portfolio_turnover <- sum(abs(weights_t2 - weights_t1)) / 2
  return(portfolio_turnover)
}
```

```
# Python
def portfolio_turnover(weights_t1, weights_t2):
    portfolio_turnover = np.sum(np.abs(weights_t2 - weights_t1)) / 2
    return portfolio_turnover
```

Example

```
# R
weights_t1 <- c(0.3, 0.4, 0.3)
weights_t2 <- c(0.2, 0.45, 0.35)
portfolio_turnover <- function(weights_t1, weights_t2) {
  portfolio_turnover <- sum(abs(weights_t2 - weights_t1)) / 2
```

```r
  return(portfolio_turnover)
}
result <- portfolio_turnover(weights_t1, weights_t2)
print(result)
```

```python
# Python
import numpy as np
weights_t1 = np.array([0.3, 0.4, 0.3])
weights_t2 = np.array([0.2, 0.45, 0.35])
def portfolio_turnover(weights_t1, weights_t2):
    portfolio_turnover = np.sum(np.abs(weights_t2 - weights_t1)) / 2
    return portfolio_turnover
result = portfolio_turnover(weights_t1, weights_t2)
print(result)
```

Output
R
[1] 0.1
Python
0.09999999999999998

20. Portfolio Rebalancing

Rebalancing a portfolio is the act of adjusting an investment portfolio's asset weights to preserve the planned asset allocation. Buying or selling assets is the process of rebalancing a portfolio to return it to its intended allocation.

```r
# R
portfolio_rebalance        <-        function(weights_initial,        returns,
rebalance_period) {
  portfolio_weights <- matrix(NA, ncol = length(weights_initial), nrow =
length(returns))
  for (i in 1:length(returns)) {
   if (i %% rebalance_period == 1 || i == 1) {
    weights_current = weights_initial
   } else {
    weights_current = portfolio_weights[i - 1, ] * (1 + returns[i - 1])
    weights_current = weights_current / sum(weights_current)
   }
   portfolio_weights[i, ] = weights_current
  }
```

```r
  return(portfolio_weights)
}
```

```python
# Python
def portfolio_rebalance(weights_initial, returns, rebalance_period):
  portfolio_weights = np.zeros((len(returns), len(weights_initial)))
  for i in range(len(returns)):
    if (i % rebalance_period == 0) or (i == 0):
      weights_current = weights_initial
    else:
      weights_current = portfolio_weights[i - 1, :] * (1 + returns[i - 1])
      weights_current /= np.sum(weights_current)
    portfolio_weights[i, :] = weights_current
  return portfolio_weights
```

Example

```r
# R
weights_initial <- c(0.3, 0.4, 0.3)
returns <- c(0.1, 0.05, 0.03, -0.02, 0.04)
rebalance_period <- 2
portfolio_rebalance <- function(weights_initial, returns,
rebalance_period) {
 portfolio_weights <- matrix(NA, ncol = length(weights_initial), nrow =
length(returns))
 for (i in 1:length(returns)) {
  if (i %% rebalance_period == 1 || i == 1) {
   weights_current = weights_initial
  } else {
   weights_current = portfolio_weights[i - 1, ] * (1 + returns[i - 1])
   weights_current = weights_current / sum(weights_current)
  }
  portfolio_weights[i, ] = weights_current
 }
 return(portfolio_weights)
}
result <- portfolio_rebalance(weights_initial, returns, rebalance_period)
print(result)
```

```python
# Python
import numpy as np
weights_initial = np.array([0.3, 0.4, 0.3])
returns = np.array([0.1, 0.05, 0.03, -0.02, 0.04])
```

```
rebalance_period = 2
def portfolio_rebalance(weights_initial, returns, rebalance_period):
    portfolio_weights = np.zeros((len(returns), len(weights_initial)))
    for i in range(len(returns)):
        if (i % rebalance_period == 0) or (i == 0):
            weights_current = weights_initial
        else:
            weights_current = portfolio_weights[i - 1, :] * (1 + returns[i - 1])
            weights_current /= np.sum(weights_current)
        portfolio_weights[i, :] = weights_current
    return portfolio_weights
result = portfolio_rebalance(weights_initial, returns, rebalance_period)
print(result)
```

Output

R

```
     [,1] [,2] [,3]
[1,]  0.3  0.4  0.3
[2,]  0.3  0.4  0.3
[3,]  0.3  0.4  0.3
[4,]  0.3  0.4  0.3
[5,]  0.3  0.4  0.3
```

Python
```
[[0.3 0.4 0.3]
 [0.3 0.4 0.3]
 [0.3 0.4 0.3]
 [0.3 0.4 0.3]
 [0.3 0.4 0.3]]
```

CHAPTER 4

20 commonly used code examples for making investment decisions in both R and Python:

1. Net Present Value (NPV)

Net present value (NPV) is used to assess how profitable a project or investment is. It calculates the difference over time between the present value of cash inflows and outflows.

```R
# R
npv <- function(cash_flows, discount_rate) {
 npv_value <- sum(cash_flows / (1 +
discount_rate)^(1:length(cash_flows)))
 return(npv_value)
}
```

```Python
# Python
def npv(cash_flows, discount_rate):
    npv_value = np.sum(cash_flows / (1 + discount_rate) ** np.arange(1,
len(cash_flows) + 1))
    return npv_value
```

Example

```R
# R
cash_flows <- c(100, 200, 300, 400, 500)
discount_rate <- 0.05
npv <- function(cash_flows, discount_rate) {
 npv_value <- sum(cash_flows / (1 +
discount_rate)^(1:length(cash_flows)))
 return(npv_value)
}
result <- npv(cash_flows, discount_rate)
print(result)
```

```Python
# Python
import numpy as np
```

```
cash_flows = np.array([100, 200, 300, 400, 500])
discount_rate = 0.05
def npv(cash_flows, discount_rate):
    npv_value = np.sum(cash_flows / (1 + discount_rate) ** np.arange(1,
len(cash_flows) + 1))
    return npv_value
result = npv(cash_flows, discount_rate)
print(result)
```

Output
R
[1] 1256.639
Python
1256.63934364013

2. Internal Rate of Return (IRR)

Internal rate of return (IRR) is used to evaluate how profitable a project
or investment is. It is a representation of the discount rate at which the
cash inflows and outflows have the same net present value. It is the rate
of return at which the present value of all future cash flows is zero.

```
# R
irr <- function(cash_flows) {
 irr_value <- uniroot(function(rate) sum(cash_flows / (1 +
rate)^(1:length(cash_flows))) - 0, c(0, 1))$root
 return(irr_value)
}
```

```
# Python
from scipy.optimize import root_scalar
def irr(cash_flows):
    irr_value = root_scalar(lambda rate: np.sum(cash_flows / (1 + rate) **
np.arange(1, len(cash_flows) + 1)) - 0, bracket=[0, 1]).root
    return irr_value
```

Example

```
# R
cash_flows <- c(-100, 20, 30, 40, 50, 60)
irr <- function(cash_flows) {
```

```r
  irr_value <- uniroot(function(rate) sum(cash_flows / (1 +
rate)^(1:length(cash_flows))) - 0, c(0, 1))$root
  return(irr_value)
}
result <- irr(cash_flows)
print(result)
```

```python
# Python
import numpy as np
from scipy.optimize import root_scalar
cash_flows = np.array([-100, 20, 30, 40, 50, 60])
def irr(cash_flows):
    irr_value = root_scalar(lambda rate: np.sum(cash_flows / (1 + rate) **
np.arange(1, len(cash_flows) + 1)) - 0, bracket=[0, 1]).root
    return irr_value
result = irr(cash_flows)
print(result)
```

Output
R
[1] 0.2328979
Python
0.23291940737673397

3. Payback Period

The payback period is used to assess how long it will take an investment to recover its initial investment. The breakeven point is the amount of time needed for an investment's total cash inflows to equal its total cash outflows.

```r
# R
payback_period <- function(cash_flows) {
  cumulative_cash_flows <- cumsum(cash_flows)
  payback_index <- which(cumulative_cash_flows >= 0)[1]
  payback_period <- ifelse(payback_index > 1, payback_index - 1 +
(cumulative_cash_flows[payback_index          -          1]          /
cash_flows[payback_index]), payback_index)
  return(payback_period)
}
```

117

```python
# Python
def payback_period(cash_flows):
    cumulative_cash_flows = np.cumsum(cash_flows)
    payback_index = np.where(cumulative_cash_flows >= 0)[0][0]
    if payback_index > 0:
        payback_period = payback_index - 1 +
(cumulative_cash_flows[payback_index - 1] /
cash_flows[payback_index])
    else:
        payback_period = payback_index
    return payback_period
```

Example

```r
# R Example
cash_flows_r <- c(-150, 50, 60, 70, 80)
payback_period_r <- function(cash_flows) {
 cumulative_cash_flows <- cumsum(cash_flows)
 payback_index <- which(cumulative_cash_flows >= 0)[1]
 if (payback_index == 1) {
  return(payback_index)
 } else {
  payback_period <- payback_index - 1 +
abs(cumulative_cash_flows[payback_index - 1]) /
cash_flows[payback_index]
  return(payback_period)
 }
}
result_r <- payback_period_r(cash_flows_r)
print(result_r)
```

```python
# Python Example
import numpy as np
cash_flows_py = np.array([-150, 50, 60, 70, 80])
def payback_period_py(cash_flows):
    cumulative_cash_flows = np.cumsum(cash_flows)
    payback_index = np.where(cumulative_cash_flows >= 0)[0][0]
    if payback_index == 0:
        return payback_index
    elif cash_flows[payback_index] == 0:
        return payback_index
    else:
```

```
    payback_period = payback_index +
(abs(cumulative_cash_flows[payback_index - 1]) /
cash_flows[payback_index])
    return payback_period
result_py = payback_period_py(cash_flows_py)
print(result_py)
```

Output
R
[1] 3.571429
Python
3.571428571428571

4. Return on Investment (ROI)

Return on Investment is a metric used to assess how profitable or effective an investment is. It shows the relationship between an investment's return or loss and its cost. It is presented as a percentage and indicates a measure of the return generated on an investment in relation to its initial cost.

```
# R
roi <- function(initial_investment, final_value) {
 roi_value <- (final_value - initial_investment) / initial_investment
 return(roi_value)
}
```

```
# Python
def roi(initial_investment, final_value):
    roi_value = (final_value - initial_investment) / initial_investment
    return roi_value
```

Example

```
# R Example
initial_investment_r <- 10000
final_value_r <- 15000
roi_r <- function(initial_investment, final_value) {
 roi_value <- (final_value - initial_investment) / initial_investment
 return(roi_value)
}
result_r <- roi_r(initial_investment_r, final_value_r)
print(result_r)
```

```python
# Python Example
def roi(initial_investment, final_value):
    roi_value = (final_value - initial_investment) / initial_investment
    return roi_value
initial_investment_py = 10000
final_value_py = 15000
result_py = roi(initial_investment_py, final_value_py)
print(result_py)
```

Output
R
[1] 0.5
Python
0.5

5. Profitability Index (PI)

Profitability Index, or Profit Investment Ratio or Value Investment Ratio, is calculated by dividing the present value of the future cash flows by the initial investment cost. It helps in ranking and selecting projects by providing a ratio of the value created per unit of investment.

```r
# R
pi <- function(initial_investment, cash_flows, discount_rate) {
  npv_value <- sum(cash_flows / (1 + discount_rate)^(1:length(cash_flows)))
  pi_value <- npv_value / initial_investment
  return(pi_value)
}
```

```python
# Python
def pi(initial_investment, cash_flows, discount_rate):
    npv_value = np.sum(cash_flows / (1 + discount_rate) ** np.arange(1, len(cash_flows) + 1))
    pi_value = npv_value / initial_investment
    return pi_value
```

Example

```r
# R Example
initial_investment_r <- 10000
```

120

```r
cash_flows_r <- c(2000, 3000, 4000, 4000, 5000)
discount_rate_r <- 0.1
pi_r <- function(initial_investment, cash_flows, discount_rate) {
  npv_value        <-        sum(cash_flows        /        (1        +
discount_rate)^(1:length(cash_flows)))
  pi_value <- npv_value / initial_investment
  return(pi_value)
}
result_r <- pi_r(initial_investment_r, cash_flows_r, discount_rate_r)
print(result_r)

# Python Example
import numpy as np
initial_investment_py = 10000
cash_flows_py = np.array([2000, 3000, 4000, 4000, 5000])
discount_rate_py = 0.1
def pi(initial_investment, cash_flows, discount_rate):
    npv_value = np.sum(cash_flows / (1 + discount_rate) ** np.arange(1,
len(cash_flows) + 1))
    pi_value = npv_value / initial_investment
    return pi_value
result_py = pi(initial_investment_py, cash_flows_py, discount_rate_py)
print(result_py)
```

Output
R
[1] 1.313944
Python
1.3139440301519394

6. Holding Period Return (HPR)

Holding Period Return is used to measure the total return an investor earns or loses on an investment during the time it is held. It considers both the capital gain (or loss) and any income generated from the investment, such as dividends or interest.

```r
# R
hpr <- function(initial_value, final_value, cash_flows) {
  hpr_value <- (final_value + sum(cash_flows)) / initial_value - 1
  return(hpr_value)
}
```

```python
# Python
def hpr(initial_value, final_value, cash_flows):
    hpr_value = (final_value + np.sum(cash_flows)) / initial_value - 1
    return hpr_value
```

Example

```r
# R Example
initial_value_r <- 10000
final_value_r <- 15000
cash_flows_r <- c(2000, 3000, 4000, 4000, 5000)
hpr_r <- function(initial_value, final_value, cash_flows) {
  hpr_value <- (final_value + sum(cash_flows)) / initial_value - 1
  return(hpr_value)
}
result_r <- hpr_r(initial_value_r, final_value_r, cash_flows_r)
print(result_r)
```

```python
# Python Example
import numpy as np
initial_value_py = 10000
final_value_py = 15000
cash_flows_py = np.array([2000, 3000, 4000, 4000, 5000])
def hpr(initial_value, final_value, cash_flows):
    hpr_value = (final_value + np.sum(cash_flows)) / initial_value - 1
    return hpr_value
result_py = hpr(initial_value_py, final_value_py, cash_flows_py)
print(result_py)
```

Output
R
[1] 2.3
Python
2.3

7. Sharpe Ratio

The Sharpe Ratio measures the risk-adjusted performance of an investment, portfolio, or strategy.

R

```r
sharpe_ratio <- function(portfolio_return, risk_free_rate,
portfolio_volatility) {
  sharpe_ratio_value <- (portfolio_return - risk_free_rate) /
portfolio_volatility
  return(sharpe_ratio_value)
}
```

```python
# Python
def sharpe_ratio(portfolio_return, risk_free_rate, portfolio_volatility):
    sharpe_ratio_value = (portfolio_return - risk_free_rate) /
portfolio_volatility
    return sharpe_ratio_value
```

Example

```r
# R Example
portfolio_return_r <- 0.1
risk_free_rate_r <- 0.05
portfolio_volatility_r <- 0.12
sharpe_ratio_r <- function(portfolio_return, risk_free_rate,
portfolio_volatility) {
  sharpe_ratio_value <- (portfolio_return - risk_free_rate) /
portfolio_volatility
  return(sharpe_ratio_value)
}
result_r <- sharpe_ratio_r(portfolio_return_r, risk_free_rate_r,
portfolio_volatility_r)
print(result_r)
```

```python
# Python Example
def sharpe_ratio(portfolio_return, risk_free_rate, portfolio_volatility):
    sharpe_ratio_value = (portfolio_return - risk_free_rate) /
portfolio_volatility
    return sharpe_ratio_value
portfolio_return_py = 0.1
risk_free_rate_py = 0.05
portfolio_volatility_py = 0.12
result_py = sharpe_ratio(portfolio_return_py, risk_free_rate_py,
portfolio_volatility_py)
print(result_py)
```

Output
R
[1] 0.4166667
Python
0.4166666666666667

8. Treynor Ratio

The Sharpe Ratio measures the risk-adjusted performance of a portfolio.

```
# R
treynor_ratio <- function(portfolio_return, risk_free_rate, beta) {
  treynor_ratio_value <- (portfolio_return - risk_free_rate) / beta
  return(treynor_ratio_value)
}
```

```
# Python
def treynor_ratio(portfolio_return, risk_free_rate, beta):
    treynor_ratio_value = (portfolio_return - risk_free_rate) / beta
    return treynor_ratio_value
```

Example

```
# R Example
portfolio_return_r <- 0.15
risk_free_rate_r <- 0.05
beta_r <- 1.2
treynor_ratio_r <- function(portfolio_return, risk_free_rate, beta) {
  treynor_ratio_value <- (portfolio_return - risk_free_rate) / beta
  return(treynor_ratio_value)
}
result_r <- treynor_ratio_r(portfolio_return_r, risk_free_rate_r, beta_r)
print(result_r)
```

```
# Python Example
def treynor_ratio(portfolio_return, risk_free_rate, beta):
    treynor_ratio_value = (portfolio_return - risk_free_rate) / beta
    return treynor_ratio_value
portfolio_return_py = 0.15
risk_free_rate_py = 0.05
beta_py = 1.2
```

124

```
result_py  =  treynor_ratio(portfolio_return_py,  risk_free_rate_py,
beta_py)
print(result_py)
```

Output
R [1] 0.08333333
Python
0.08333333333333333

9. Sortino Ratio

The Sortino Ratio is the risk-adjusted performance of an investment by focusing specifically on the downside risk.

```
# R
sortino_ratio <- function(portfolio_return, risk_free_rate,
downside_deviation) {
  sortino_ratio_value <- (portfolio_return - risk_free_rate) /
downside_deviation
  return(sortino_ratio_value)
}
```

```
# Python
def sortino_ratio(portfolio_return, risk_free_rate, downside_deviation):
    sortino_ratio_value = (portfolio_return - risk_free_rate) /
downside_deviation
    return sortino_ratio_value
```

Another Example

```
# R Example
portfolio_return_r <- 0.12
risk_free_rate_r <- 0.03
downside_deviation_r <- 0.08
sortino_ratio_r <- function(portfolio_return, risk_free_rate,
downside_deviation) {
  sortino_ratio_value <- (portfolio_return - risk_free_rate) /
downside_deviation
  return(sortino_ratio_value)
}
result_r <- sortino_ratio_r(portfolio_return_r, risk_free_rate_r,
downside_deviation_r)
```

```
print(result_r)

# Python Example
def sortino_ratio(portfolio_return, risk_free_rate, downside_deviation):
    sortino_ratio_value = (portfolio_return - risk_free_rate) /
downside_deviation
    return sortino_ratio_value
portfolio_return_py = 0.12
risk_free_rate_py = 0.03
downside_deviation_py = 0.08
result_py = sortino_ratio(portfolio_return_py, risk_free_rate_py,
downside_deviation_py)
print(result_py)
```

Output
R
[1] 1.125
Python
1.125

10. Conditional Value-at-Risk (CVaR)

Another Example for (CVar)

```
# R Example
returns_r <- c(0.1, 0.05, 0.01, -0.02, -0.04, -0.08, -0.1, -0.12, -0.15)
alpha_r <- 0.05
cvar_r <- function(returns, alpha) {
 cvar_value <- quantile(returns, probs = alpha)
 return(cvar_value)
}
result_r <- cvar_r(returns_r, alpha_r)
print(result_r)
```

```
# Python Example
import numpy as np
returns_py = np.array([0.1, 0.05, 0.01, -0.02, -0.04, -0.08, -0.1, -0.12, -0.15])
alpha_py = 0.05
def cvar(returns, alpha):
    cvar_value = np.percentile(returns, q=100 * alpha)
    return cvar_value
```

```
result_py = cvar(returns_py, alpha_py)
print(result_py)
```

Output
```
R
  5%
-0.138
Python
-0.13799999999999998
```

11. Value-at-Risk (VaR)

Another Example for (Var)

```
# R Example
returns_r <- c(0.1, 0.05, 0.01, -0.02, -0.04, -0.08, -0.1, -0.12, -0.15)
alpha_r <- 0.05
var_r <- function(returns, alpha) {
 var_value <- quantile(returns, probs = alpha)
 return(var_value)
}
result_r <- var_r(returns_r, alpha_r)
print(result_r)

# Python Example
import numpy as np
returns_py = np.array([0.1, 0.05, 0.01, -0.02, -0.04, -0.08, -0.1, -0.12, -0.15])
alpha_py = 0.05
def var(returns, alpha):
   var_value = np.percentile(returns, q=100 * alpha)
   return var_value
result_py = var(returns_py, alpha_py)
print(result_py)
```

Output
```
R
-0.138
Python
-0.13799999999999998
```

12. Maximum Drawdown

Maximum Drawdown represents the largest percentage decline or loss from a peak value to a trough value in an investment portfolio or asset over a specific period.

```
# R Example
returns_r <- c(0.1, -0.05, 0.01, -0.02, -0.04, 0.02, -0.03, -0.02, 0.01)
max_drawdown_r <- function(returns) {
  cum_returns <- cumprod(1 + returns)
  peak <- cummax(cum_returns)
  drawdown <- (cum_returns - peak) / peak
  max_drawdown_value <- max(drawdown)
  return(max_drawdown_value)
}
result_r <- max_drawdown_r(returns_r)
print(result_r)
```

```
# Python Example
import numpy as np
returns_py = np.array([0.1, -0.05, 0.01, -0.02, -0.04, 0.02, -0.03, -0.02, 0.01])
def max_drawdown(returns):
    cum_returns = np.cumprod(1 + returns)
    peak = np.maximum.accumulate(cum_returns)
    drawdown = (cum_returns - peak) / peak
    max_drawdown_value = np.max(drawdown)
    return max_drawdown_value
result_py = max_drawdown(returns_py)
print(result_py)
```

Output
R 0, Python 0.0

13. Capital Asset Pricing Model (CAPM) Beta

Another Example for CAPM beta

```
# R Example
stock_returns_r <- c(0.04, 0.05, 0.02, 0.03, 0.01)
market_returns_r <- c(0.03, 0.02, 0.01, 0.02, 0.01)
```

```r
capm_beta_r <- function(stock_returns, market_returns) {
  cov_value <- cov(stock_returns, market_returns)
  var_value <- var(market_returns)
  beta <- cov_value / var_value
  return(beta)
}
result_r <- capm_beta_r(stock_returns_r, market_returns_r)
print(result_r)
```

```python
# Python Example
import numpy as np
stock_returns_py = np.array([0.04, 0.05, 0.02, 0.03, 0.01])
market_returns_py = np.array([0.03, 0.02, 0.01, 0.02, 0.01])
def capm_beta(stock_returns, market_returns):
    cov_value = np.cov(stock_returns, market_returns)[0][1]
    var_value = np.var(market_returns)
    beta = cov_value / var_value
    return beta
result_py = capm_beta(stock_returns_py, market_returns_py)
print(result_py)
```

Output
R
[1] 1.428571
Python
1.7857142857142858

14. Jensen's Alpha

Another Example for Alpha

```r
# R
portfolio_return <- 0.08
risk_free_rate <- 0.02
portfolio_beta <- 1.2
benchmark_return <- 0.06
jensens_alpha <- function(portfolio_return, risk_free_rate, portfolio_beta, benchmark_return) {
  jensens_alpha_value <- portfolio_return - (risk_free_rate + portfolio_beta * (benchmark_return - risk_free_rate))
  return(jensens_alpha_value)
}
```

```
result_r <- jensens_alpha(portfolio_return, risk_free_rate, portfolio_beta,
benchmark_return)
print(result_r)

# Python
def jensens_alpha(portfolio_return, risk_free_rate, portfolio_beta,
benchmark_return):
  jensens_alpha_value = portfolio_return - (risk_free_rate +
portfolio_beta * (benchmark_return - risk_free_rate))
  return jensens_alpha_value
portfolio_return = 0.08
risk_free_rate = 0.02
portfolio_beta = 1.2
benchmark_return = 0.06
result_py = jensens_alpha(portfolio_return, risk_free_rate,
portfolio_beta, benchmark_return)
print(result_py)
```

Output
R
[1] 0.012
Python
0.01200000000000001

15. Modigliani Ratio

An asset or investment portfolio's risk-adjusted performance is evaluated
using the Modigliani Ratio. It divides the performance of an investment
into two parts: residual risk and market risk.

```
# R
modigliani_ratio <- function(portfolio_return, benchmark_return,
portfolio_volatility) {
  modigliani_ratio_value <- (portfolio_return - benchmark_return) /
portfolio_volatility
  return(modigliani_ratio_value)
}
```

```
# Python
def modigliani_ratio(portfolio_return, benchmark_return,
portfolio_volatility):
```

```
  modigliani_ratio_value = (portfolio_return - benchmark_return) /
portfolio_volatility
  return modigliani_ratio_value
```

Example

```r
# R
portfolio_return <- 0.1
benchmark_return <- 0.08
portfolio_volatility <- 0.15
modigliani_ratio <- function(portfolio_return, benchmark_return,
portfolio_volatility) {
 modigliani_ratio_value <- (portfolio_return - benchmark_return) /
portfolio_volatility
 return(modigliani_ratio_value)
}
result_r <- modigliani_ratio(portfolio_return, benchmark_return,
portfolio_volatility)
print(result_r)
```

```python
# Python
def modigliani_ratio(portfolio_return, benchmark_return,
portfolio_volatility):
  modigliani_ratio_value = (portfolio_return - benchmark_return) /
portfolio_volatility
  return modigliani_ratio_value
portfolio_return = 0.1
benchmark_return = 0.08
portfolio_volatility = 0.15
result_py  =  modigliani_ratio(portfolio_return,  benchmark_return,
portfolio_volatility)
print(result_py)
```

Output
R
[1] 0.1333333
Python
0.13333333333333336

16. Information Ratio

The Information Ratio takes tracking inaccuracy into account when calculating the risk-adjusted performance of an active return portfolio. It is frequently used to evaluate how well an investment manager or portfolio generates excess returns in comparison to a benchmark while taking volatility and risk into account.

```r
# R
information_ratio <- function(active_returns, tracking_error) {
  information_ratio_value <- mean(active_returns) / tracking_error
  return(information_ratio_value)
}
```

```python
# Python
def information_ratio(active_returns, tracking_error):
    information_ratio_value = np.mean(active_returns) / tracking_error
    return information_ratio_value
```

Example

```r
# R
active_returns <- c(0.04, 0.05, 0.02, 0.03, 0.01)
tracking_error <- 0.02
information_ratio <- function(active_returns, tracking_error) {
  information_ratio_value <- mean(active_returns) / tracking_error
  return(information_ratio_value)
}
result_r <- information_ratio(active_returns, tracking_error)
print(result_r)
```

```python
# Python
import numpy as np
active_returns = np.array([0.04, 0.05, 0.02, 0.03, 0.01])
tracking_error = 0.02
def information_ratio(active_returns, tracking_error):
    information_ratio_value = np.mean(active_returns) / tracking_error
    return information_ratio_value
result_py = information_ratio(active_returns, tracking_error)
print(result_py)
```

Output
R
[1] 1.5
Python
1.5000000000000002

17. Portfolio Turnover

A financial indicator called portfolio turnover calculates how frequently assets in a portfolio are purchased and sold over a given time frame.

```r
# R
portfolio_turnover <- function(weights_t1, weights_t2) {
  portfolio_turnover_value <- sum(abs(weights_t2 - weights_t1)) / 2
  return(portfolio_turnover_value)
}
```

```python
# Python
def portfolio_turnover(weights_t1, weights_t2):
    portfolio_turnover_value = np.sum(np.abs(weights_t2 - weights_t1)) / 2
    return portfolio_turnover_value
```

Example

```r
# R
weights_t1 <- c(0.2, 0.3, 0.5)
weights_t2 <- c(0.3, 0.3, 0.4)
portfolio_turnover <- function(weights_t1, weights_t2) {
  portfolio_turnover_value <- sum(abs(weights_t2 - weights_t1)) / 2
  return(portfolio_turnover_value)
}
result_r <- portfolio_turnover(weights_t1, weights_t2)
print(result_r)
```

```python
# Python
import numpy as np
weights_t1 = np.array([0.2, 0.3, 0.5])
weights_t2 = np.array([0.3, 0.3, 0.4])
def portfolio_turnover(weights_t1, weights_t2):
    portfolio_turnover_value = np.sum(np.abs(weights_t2 - weights_t1)) / 2
```

```
   return portfolio_turnover_value
result_py = portfolio_turnover(weights_t1, weights_t2)
print(result_py)
```

Output
R
[1] 0.1
Python
0.09999999999999998

18. Portfolio Rebalancing

The practice of changing an asset's weight in a portfolio to preserve the intended asset allocation is known as portfolio rebalancing. Rebalancing aims to return the portfolio to its initial or target asset allocation, making sure that it is in line with the investor's overall strategy, investing objectives, and risk tolerance.

```
# R
portfolio_rebalance <- function(weights_initial, returns,
rebalance_period) {
 portfolio_weights <- matrix(NA, ncol = length(weights_initial), nrow =
length(returns))
 for (i in 1:length(returns)) {
  if (i %% rebalance_period == 1 || i == 1) {
   weights_current = weights_initial
  } else {
   weights_current = portfolio_weights[i - 1, ] * (1 + returns[i - 1])
   weights_current = weights_current / sum(weights_current)
  }
  portfolio_weights[i, ] = weights_current
 }
 return(portfolio_weights)
}
```

```
# Python
def portfolio_rebalance(weights_initial, returns, rebalance_period):
   portfolio_weights = np.zeros((len(returns), len(weights_initial)))
   for i in range(len(returns)):
      if (i % rebalance_period == 0) or (i == 0):
         weights_current = weights_initial
```

```
    else:
      weights_current = portfolio_weights[i - 1, :] * (1 + returns[i - 1])
      weights_current /= np.sum(weights_current)
    portfolio_weights[i, :] = weights_current
  return portfolio_weights
```

Example

```R
# R
weights_initial <- c(0.3, 0.4, 0.3)
returns <- c(0.05, 0.02, 0.03, 0.01, 0.04)
rebalance_period <- 2
portfolio_rebalance      <-      function(weights_initial,      returns,
rebalance_period) {
  portfolio_weights <- matrix(NA, ncol = length(weights_initial), nrow =
length(returns))
  for (i in 1:length(returns)) {
   if (i %% rebalance_period == 1 || i == 1) {
    weights_current = weights_initial
   } else {
    weights_current = portfolio_weights[i - 1, ] * (1 + returns[i - 1])
    weights_current = weights_current / sum(weights_current)
   }
   portfolio_weights[i, ] = weights_current
  }
  return(portfolio_weights)
}
result_r      <-      portfolio_rebalance(weights_initial,      returns,
rebalance_period)
print(result_r)
```

```python
# Python
import numpy as np
weights_initial = np.array([0.3, 0.4, 0.3])
returns = np.array([0.05, 0.02, 0.03, 0.01, 0.04])
rebalance_period = 2
def portfolio_rebalance(weights_initial, returns, rebalance_period):
    portfolio_weights = np.zeros((len(returns), len(weights_initial)))
    for i in range(len(returns)):
        if (i % rebalance_period == 0) or (i == 0):
            weights_current = weights_initial
        else:
```

```
        weights_current = portfolio_weights[i - 1, :] * (1 + returns[i - 1])
        weights_current /= np.sum(weights_current)
    portfolio_weights[i, :] = weights_current
  return portfolio_weights
result_py      =      portfolio_rebalance(weights_initial,      returns,
rebalance_period)
print(result_py)
```

Output
R
```
    [,1] [,2] [,3]
[1,]  0.3  0.4  0.3
[2,]  0.3  0.4  0.3
[3,]  0.3  0.4  0.3
[4,]  0.3  0.4  0.3
[5,]  0.3  0.4  0.3
```
Python
```
[[0.3 0.4 0.3]
 [0.3 0.4 0.3]
 [0.3 0.4 0.3]
 [0.3 0.4 0.3]
 [0.3 0.4 0.3]]
```

19. Mean-Variance Optimization

Mean-Variance Optimization aims to construct an optimal portfolio by
considering the trade-off between expected return and portfolio volatility.
It is to identify a portfolio that maximizes expected return for a given level
of risk or minimizes risk for a targeted level of expected return.

```
# R
library(quadprog)
mean_variance_optimization <- function(cov_matrix, expected_returns,
risk_aversion) {
  A <- 2 * cov_matrix
  b <- rep(0, nrow(cov_matrix))
  C <- -expected_returns
  Dmat <- chol(A, pivot = TRUE)
  Dinv <- solve(Dmat)
  Amat <- t(Dinv) %*% Dinv
  bvec <- t(Dinv) %*% b
```

```r
 sol <- solve.QP(Dmat = Amat, dvec = bvec, Amat = matrix(1, nrow =
1), bvec = matrix(1, nrow = 1), meq = 1)
 optimal_weights <- sol$solution
 return(optimal_weights)
}
```

```python
# Python
from scipy.optimize import minimize
def mean_variance_optimization(cov_matrix, expected_returns,
risk_aversion):
   n_assets = len(expected_returns)
   initial_weights = np.ones(n_assets) / n_assets
   bounds = [(0, 1) for _ in range(n_assets)]
   def objective(weights):
      portfolio_return = np.sum(expected_returns * weights)
      portfolio_volatility = np.sqrt(np.dot(weights.T, np.dot(cov_matrix,
weights)))
      utility = portfolio_return - risk_aversion * (portfolio_volatility **
2)
      return -utility
   result = minimize(objective, initial_weights, method='SLSQP',
bounds=bounds, constraints={'type': 'eq', 'fun': lambda weights:
np.sum(weights) - 1})
   optimal_weights = result.x
   return optimal_weights
```

Example

```r
# R
library(quadprog)
mean_variance_optimization <- function(cov_matrix, expected_returns,
risk_aversion) {
 A <- 2 * cov_matrix
 b <- rep(0, nrow(cov_matrix))
 C <- -expected_returns
 Dmat <- chol(A, pivot = TRUE)
 Dinv <- solve(Dmat)
 Amat <- t(Dinv) %*% Dinv
 bvec <- t(Dinv) %*% b
 sol <- solve.QP(Dmat = Amat, dvec = bvec, Amat = matrix(1, nrow =
1), bvec = matrix(1, nrow = 1), meq = 1)
 optimal_weights <- sol$solution
```

```r
  return(optimal_weights)
}
# Example usage
cov_matrix <- matrix(c(0.1, 0.02, 0.01, 0.02, 0.12, 0.05, 0.01, 0.05, 0.1),
nrow = 3, byrow = TRUE)
expected_returns <- c(0.05, 0.08, 0.12)
risk_aversion <- 0.1
result_r <- mean_variance_optimization(cov_matrix, expected_returns,
risk_aversion)
print(result_r)
```

```python
# Python
import numpy as np
from scipy.optimize import minimize
def mean_variance_optimization(cov_matrix, expected_returns,
risk_aversion):
  n_assets = len(expected_returns)
  initial_weights = np.ones(n_assets) / n_assets
  bounds = [(0, 1) for _ in range(n_assets)]
  def objective(weights):
    portfolio_return = np.sum(expected_returns * weights)
    portfolio_volatility = np.sqrt(np.dot(weights.T, np.dot(cov_matrix,
weights)))
    utility = portfolio_return - risk_aversion * (portfolio_volatility **
2)
    return -utility
  result = minimize(objective, initial_weights, method='SLSQP',
bounds=bounds, constraints={'type': 'eq', 'fun': lambda weights:
np.sum(weights) - 1})
  optimal_weights = result.x
  return optimal_weights
# Example usage
cov_matrix = np.array([[0.1, 0.02, 0.01], [0.02, 0.12, 0.05], [0.01, 0.05,
0.1]])
expected_returns = np.array([0.05, 0.08, 0.12])
risk_aversion = 0.1
result_py = mean_variance_optimization(cov_matrix, expected_returns,
risk_aversion)
print(result_py)
```

Output
R

```
       [,1] [,2] [,3]
[1,]   0.3  0.4  0.3
[2,]   0.3  0.4  0.3
[3,]   0.3  0.4  0.3
[4,]   0.3  0.4  0.3
[5,]   0.3  0.4  0.3
```
Python
```
[1.12172823e-16 1.11022302e-16 1.00000000e+00]
```

20. Portfolio Risk and Return

The level of unpredictability or variability connected to the possible returns of a group of assets is known as portfolio risk. A portfolio's return, represented as a percentage of the initial investment, is the profit or loss realized on a group of assets over a given time.

```
# R
cov_matrix <- matrix(c(0.05, 0.006, 0.006, 0.01), nrow = 2, byrow = TRUE)
weights <- c(0.4, 0.6)
expected_returns <- c(0.08, 0.12)
# Portfolio Return
portfolio_return <- sum(weights * expected_returns)
# Portfolio Risk
portfolio_risk <- sqrt(t(weights) %*% cov_matrix %*% weights)
print(paste("Portfolio Return:", portfolio_return))
print(paste("Portfolio Risk:", portfolio_risk))
```

```
# Python
import numpy as np
cov_matrix = np.array([[0.05, 0.006], [0.006, 0.01]])
weights = np.array([0.4, 0.6])
expected_returns = np.array([0.08, 0.12])
# Portfolio Return
portfolio_return = np.sum(weights * expected_returns)
# Portfolio Risk
portfolio_risk = np.sqrt(weights.T @ cov_matrix @ weights)
print(f"Portfolio Return: {portfolio_return}")
print(f"Portfolio Risk: {portfolio_risk}")
```

Output
R
[1] "Portfolio Return: 0.104"
[1] "Portfolio Risk: 0.120332871651931"
Python
Portfolio Return: 0.104
Portfolio Risk: 0.1203328716519306

CHAPTER 5

This chapters covers 20 commonly used code examples for working with interest rates and time value of money calculations in both R and Python:

1. Future Value (FV)

Future Value represents the estimated value of an investment or cash flow at a specified future point in time, considering the effects of compounding. The key components influencing future value include the initial principal amount invested or saved, the interest rate or return earned on the investment, and the time over which the investment compounds.

```r
# R
fv <- function(pv, rate, n) {
  fv_value <- pv * (1 + rate)^n
  return(fv_value)
}
# Example
pv <- 1000
rate <- 0.05
n <- 10
fv_value <- fv(pv, rate, n)
fv_value
```

```python
# Python
def fv(pv, rate, n):
    fv_value = pv * (1 + rate)**n
    return fv_value
# Example
pv = 1000
rate = 0.05
n = 10
fv_value = fv(pv, rate, n)
print(fv_value)
```

Output
R [1] 1628.895
Python 1628.894626777442

2. Present Value (PV)

Present Value is the current worth of a future sum of money, considering the time value of money. The key components of present value include the future cash flow or sum of money, the discount rate (interest rate or required rate of return), and the time over which the discounting occurs.

```r
# R
pv <- function(fv, rate, n) {
  pv_value <- fv / (1 + rate)^n
  return(pv_value)
}
# Example in R
pv_value_r <- pv(1500, 0.04, 6)
print(pv_value_r)
```

```python
# Python
def pv(fv, rate, n):
    pv_value = fv / (1 + rate)**n
    return pv_value
# Example in Python
pv_value_py = pv(1500, 0.04, 6)
print(pv_value_py)
```

Output
R
[1] 1185.472
Python
1185.4717885952186

3. Compound Interest

Compound Interest refers to the interest earned on both the initial principal and any accumulated interest from previous periods.

```r
# R
compound_interest <- function(pv, rate, n) {
  compound_interest_value <- pv * (1 + rate)^n - pv
  return(compound_interest_value)
}
```

```
# Example in R
compound_interest_value_r <- compound_interest(1000, 0.05, 3)
print(compound_interest_value_r)

# Python
def compound_interest(pv, rate, n):
    compound_interest_value = pv * (1 + rate)**n - pv
    return compound_interest_value
# Example in Python
compound_interest_value_py = compound_interest(1000, 0.05, 3)
print(compound_interest_value_py)
```

Output
R
[1] 157.625
Python
157.62500000000023

4. Simple Interest

Simple Interest is calculating interest on a loan or investment based solely on the initial principal amount. The key components of simple interest include the principal amount, the interest rate, and the time for which the interest is calculated.

```
# R
simple_interest <- function(pv, rate, n) {
 simple_interest_value <- pv * rate * n
 return(simple_interest_value)
}
# Example in R
simple_interest_value_r <- simple_interest(1000, 0.05, 3)
print(simple_interest_value_r)

# Python
def simple_interest(pv, rate, n):
    simple_interest_value = pv * rate * n
    return simple_interest_value
# Example in Python
simple_interest_value_py = simple_interest(1000, 0.05, 3)
print(simple_interest_value_py)
```

Output
R
[1] 150
Python
150.0

5. Annual Percentage Yield (APY)

Annual Percentage Yield (APY) is a standardized measure used to express the annualized rate of return on an investment, considering the effect of compounding.

```r
# R
apy <- function(rate, n) {
 apy_value <- (1 + rate / n)^n - 1
 return(apy_value)
}
# Example in R
apy_value_r <- apy(0.05, 12)
print(apy_value_r)
```

```python
# Python
def apy(rate, n):
    apy_value = (1 + rate / n)**n - 1
    return apy_value
# Example in Python
apy_value_py = apy(0.05, 12)
print(apy_value_py)
```

Output
R
[1] 0.0511619
Python
0.051161897881732976

6. Present Value of Annuity

The Present Value of an annuity represents the current worth of a series of equal payments or cash inflows that occur at regular intervals over a specified period, considering the time value of money.

```
# R
pv_annuity <- function(c, rate, n) {
  pv_annuity_value <- c * (1 - (1 + rate)^(-n)) / rate
  return(pv_annuity_value)
}
# Example in R
pv_annuity_value_r <- pv_annuity(1000, 0.05, 10)
print(pv_annuity_value_r)
```

```
# Python
def pv_annuity(c, rate, n):
    pv_annuity_value = c * (1 - (1 + rate)**(-n)) / rate
    return pv_annuity_value
# Example in Python
pv_annuity_value_py = pv_annuity(1000, 0.05, 10)
print(pv_annuity_value_py)
```

Output
R
[1] 7721.735
Python
7721.734929184818

7. Future Value of Annuity

The Future Value of an annuity represents the cumulative total of a series of equal payments or cash inflows that occur at regular intervals over a specified period.

```
# R
fv_annuity <- function(c, rate, n) {
  fv_annuity_value <- c * ((1 + rate)^n - 1) / rate
  return(fv_annuity_value)
}
# Example in R
```

```
fv_annuity_value_r <- fv_annuity(1000, 0.05, 10)
print(fv_annuity_value_r)

# Python
def fv_annuity(c, rate, n):
    fv_annuity_value = c * ((1 + rate)**n - 1) / rate
    return fv_annuity_value
# Example in Python
fv_annuity_value_py = fv_annuity(1000, 0.05, 10)
print(fv_annuity_value_py)
```

Output
R
[1] 12577.89
Python
12577.892535548839

8. Present Value of Perpetuity

The Present Value of a Perpetuity represents the current worth of an infinite series of equal payments or cash inflows that continue indefinitely.

```
# R
pv_perpetuity <- function(c, rate) {
  pv_perpetuity_value <- c / rate
  return(pv_perpetuity_value)
}
# Example in R
pv_perpetuity_value_r <- pv_perpetuity(1000, 0.05)
print(pv_perpetuity_value_r)

# Python
def pv_perpetuity(c, rate):
    pv_perpetuity_value = c / rate
    return pv_perpetuity_value
# Example in Python
pv_perpetuity_value_py = pv_perpetuity(1000, 0.05)
print(pv_perpetuity_value_py)
```

Output
R[1] 20000
Python 20000.0

9. Future Value with Continuous Compounding

The Future Value with Continuous Compounding represents the future worth of an investment or sum of money that grows continuously over time, considering the effects of compounding at every instant.

```r
# R
fv_continuous <- function(pv, rate, n) {
  fv_continuous_value <- pv * exp(rate * n)
  return(fv_continuous_value)
}
# Example in R
fv_continuous_value_r <- fv_continuous(1000, 0.05, 5)
print(fv_continuous_value_r)
```

```python
# Python
import numpy as np
def fv_continuous(pv, rate, n):
    fv_continuous_value = pv * np.exp(rate * n)
    return fv_continuous_value
# Example in Python
fv_continuous_value_py = fv_continuous(1000, 0.05, 5)
print(fv_continuous_value_py)
```

Output
R
[1] 1284.025
Python
1284.0254166877414

10. Present Value with Continuous Compounding

The Present Value with Continuous Compounding is the current worth of a future sum of money that grows continuously over time, considering the effects of compounding at every instant.

```r
# R
pv_continuous <- function(fv, rate, n) {
  pv_continuous_value <- fv / exp(rate * n)
  return(pv_continuous_value)
```

```
}
# Example in R
pv_continuous_value_r <- pv_continuous(1284.025, 0.05, 5)
print(pv_continuous_value_r)

# Python
import numpy as np
def pv_continuous(fv, rate, n):
    pv_continuous_value = fv / np.exp(rate * n)
    return pv_continuous_value
# Example in Python
pv_continuous_value_py = pv_continuous(1284.025, 0.05, 5)
print(pv_continuous_value_py)
```

Output
R
[1] 999.9997
Python
999.9996754832608

11. Effective Annual Rate (EAR)

The Effective Annual Rate (EAR) is a standardized way of expressing the annual interest rate on a financial product, accounting for the impact of compounding. Because it accounts for the frequency of compounding interest, it offers a more accurate representation of the true annual interest rate than the nominal interest rate.

```
# R
ear <- function(rate, n) {
    ear_value <- (1 + rate / n)^n - 1
    return(ear_value)
}
# Example in R
ear_value_r <- ear(0.05, 12)
print(ear_value_r)

# Python
def ear(rate, n):
    ear_value = (1 + rate / n)**n - 1
    return ear_value
# Example in Python
```

```
ear_value_py = ear(0.05, 12)
print(ear_value_py)
```

Output
R
[1] 0.0511619
Python
0.051161897881732976

12. Present Value of Growing Perpetuity

The Present Value of a Growing Perpetuity is used to calculate the current value of an infinite series of future cash flows that grow at a constant rate indefinitely. It is commonly applied to value perpetuity-like assets such as stocks that are expected to provide dividends that grow at a stable rate.

```
# R
pv_growing_perpetuity <- function(c, rate, growth_rate) {
  pv_growing_perpetuity_value <- c / (rate - growth_rate)
  return(pv_growing_perpetuity_value)
}
# Example in R
pv_value_r <- pv_growing_perpetuity(100, 0.06, 0.03)
print(pv_value_r)
```

```
# Python
def pv_growing_perpetuity(c, rate, growth_rate):
    pv_growing_perpetuity_value = c / (rate - growth_rate)
    return pv_growing_perpetuity_value
# Example in Python
pv_value_py = pv_growing_perpetuity(100, 0.06, 0.03)
print(pv_value_py)
```

Output
R
[1] 3333.333
Python
3333.3333333333335

13. Number of Periods (N)

It represents the total count of compounding periods or payment periods over the life of an investment or financial instrument.

```r
# R
n_periods <- function(pv, fv, rate) {
  n_periods_value <- log(fv / pv) / log(1 + rate)
  return(n_periods_value)
}
# Example in R
n_value_r <- n_periods(100, 200, 0.05)
print(n_value_r)
```

```python
# Python
import numpy as np
def n_periods(pv, fv, rate):
    n_periods_value = np.log(fv / pv) / np.log(1 + rate)
    return n_periods_value
# Example in Python
n_value_py = n_periods(100, 200, 0.05)
print(n_value_py)
```

Output
R
[1] 14.2067
Python
14.206699082890461

14. Effective Interest Rate for Continuous Compounding

This represents the annual interest rate when interest is compounded continuously over time. This rate provides a standardized measure that accounts for the impact of continuous compounding on the growth of an investment or loan.

```r
# R
continuous_rate <- function(ear, n) {
  continuous_rate_value <- n * (exp(ear / n) - 1)
  return(continuous_rate_value)
```

```
}
# Example in R
continuous_rate_r <- continuous_rate(0.08, 12)
print(continuous_rate_r)

# Python
import numpy as np
def continuous_rate(ear, n):
    continuous_rate_value = n * (np.exp(ear / n) - 1)
    return continuous_rate_value
# Example in Python
continuous_rate_py = continuous_rate(0.08, 12)
print(continuous_rate_py)
```

Output
R
[1] 0.08026726
Python
0.08026726024823283

15. Present Value of Growing Annuity

This represents the current worth of a series of future cash flows that increase at a constant rate over time, considering the time value of money.

```
# R
pv_growing_annuity <- function(c, rate, growth_rate, n) {
  pv_growing_annuity_value <- c * ((1 - (1 + growth_rate)^n) / (rate -
growth_rate)) / (1 + rate)^n
  return(pv_growing_annuity_value)
}
# Example in R
pv_growing_annuity_r <- pv_growing_annuity(-1500, 0.03, 0.01, 8)
print(pv_growing_annuity_r)

# Python
def pv_growing_annuity(c, rate, growth_rate, n):
    pv_growing_annuity_value = c * ((1 - (1 + growth_rate)**n) / (rate -
growth_rate)) / (1 + rate)**n
    return pv_growing_annuity_value
# Example in Python
pv_growing_annuity_py = pv_growing_annuity(-1500, 0.03, 0.01, 8)
```

```
print(pv_growing_annuity_py)
```

Output
R
[1] 4905.589
Python
4905.588641072848

16. Continuous Compounding for Continuous Rate

This concept involves compounding interest continuously over time using a rate that changes continuously. The interest on an investment or loan is calculated and added to the principal an infinite number of times, resulting in a continuous growth or decay of the investment or debt.

```
# R
continuous_compound <- function(pv, continuous_rate, n) {
  continuous_compound_value <- pv * exp(continuous_rate * n)
  return(continuous_compound_value)
}
# Example in R
continuous_compound_r <- continuous_compound(5000, 0.05, 10)
print(continuous_compound_r)
```

```
# Python
import numpy as np
def continuous_compound(pv, continuous_rate, n):
    continuous_compound_value = pv * np.exp(continuous_rate * n)
    return continuous_compound_value
# Example in Python
continuous_compound_py = continuous_compound(5000, 0.05, 10)
print(continuous_compound_py)
```

Output
R
[1] 8243.606
Python
8243.606353500641

17. Loan Payment (Amortizing Loan)

The loan payment for an amortizing loan is a periodic, fixed payment made by a borrower to a lender to repay both the principal amount and the interest on a loan over time.

```r
# R
loan_payment <- function(pv, rate, n) {
  loan_payment_value <- pv * rate / (1 - (1 + rate)^(-n))
  return(loan_payment_value)
}
# Example in R
loan_payment_r <- loan_payment(10000, 0.08, 5)
print(loan_payment_r)
```

```python
# Python
def loan_payment(pv, rate, n):
    loan_payment_value = pv * rate / (1 - (1 + rate)**(-n))
    return loan_payment_value
# Example in Python
loan_payment_py = loan_payment(10000, 0.08, 5)
print(loan_payment_py)
```

Output
R
[1] 2504.565
Python
2504.564545668364

18. Loan Balance (Amortizing Loan)

The loan balance for an amortizing loan represents the remaining amount of principal yet to be repaid at any given point in time during the loan term. As borrowers make periodic payments, a portion of each payment is applied to reduce the outstanding principal, while the remaining part covers the accrued interest.

```r
# R
loan_balance <- function(pv, rate, n, t) {
```

```r
  loan_balance_value <- pv * ((1 + rate)^t - (1 + rate)^n) / ((1 + rate)^n -
1)
  return(loan_balance_value)
}
# Example values
pv_example <- -1000
rate_example <- 0.05
n_example <- 5
t_example <- 3
loan_balance(pv_example, rate_example, n_example, t_example)
```

```python
# Python
def loan_balance(pv, rate, n, t):
    loan_balance_value = pv * ((1 + rate)**t - (1 + rate)**n) / ((1 + rate)**n
- 1)
    return loan_balance_value
# Example values
pv_example = -1000
rate_example = 0.05
n_example = 5
t_example = 3
result = loan_balance(pv_example, rate_example, n_example, t_example)
print(result)
```

Output
R
[1] 429.4769
Python
429.47694890063497

19. Loan Payoff Period (Amortizing Loan)

The loan payoff period for an amortizing loan refers to the amount of time
it takes for a borrower to fully repay the loan, covering both the principal
amount and the accrued interest, through a series of regular, fixed
payments.

```r
# R
loan_payoff_period <- function(loan_amount, annual_interest_rate,
monthly_payment) {
  remaining_balance <- loan_amount
  periods <- 0
```

```r
  while (remaining_balance > 0) {
   interest_payment <- remaining_balance * annual_interest_rate / 12
   principal_payment <- monthly_payment - interest_payment
   remaining_balance <- remaining_balance - principal_payment
   periods <- periods + 1
   if (periods > 1000) {
    break
   }
  }
  return(periods)
}
# Example usage
loan_amount <- 100000
annual_interest_rate <- 0.06
monthly_payment <- 1000
loan_payoff_period(loan_amount, annual_interest_rate,
monthly_payment)
```

```python
# Python
def loan_payoff_period(loan_amount, annual_interest_rate,
monthly_payment):
   remaining_balance = loan_amount
   periods = 0
   while remaining_balance > 0:
      interest_payment = remaining_balance * annual_interest_rate / 12
      principal_payment = monthly_payment - interest_payment
      remaining_balance = remaining_balance - principal_payment
      periods += 1
      if periods > 1000:
         break
   return periods
# Example usage
loan_amount = 100000
annual_interest_rate = 0.06
monthly_payment = 1000
result = loan_payoff_period(loan_amount, annual_interest_rate,
monthly_payment)
print(result)
```

Output
R [1] 139
Python 139

20. Loan Interest Payment (Amortizing Loan)

The loan interest payment for an amortizing loan is the portion of the regular loan payment that covers the interest charged on the remaining balance of the loan.

```r
# R
loan_interest_payment <- function(pv, rate, t) {
  loan_interest_payment_value <- pv * rate * (1 - (1 + rate)^(t - 1)) / (1 - (1 + rate)^(-t))
  return(loan_interest_payment_value)
}
# Example usage
result <- loan_interest_payment(-10000, 0.05, 5)
print(result)
```

```python
# Python
def loan_interest_payment(pv, rate, t):
    loan_interest_payment_value = pv * rate * (1 - (1 + rate)**(t - 1)) / (1 - (1 + rate)**(-t))
    return loan_interest_payment_value
# Example usage
result = loan_interest_payment(-10000, 0.05, 5)
print(result)
```

Output
R
[1] 497.7651
Python
497.76512589130095

CHAPTER 6

This chapter covers 20 commonly used code examples for foreign exchange (FX) calculations in both R and Python:

1. Convert Between Currencies

Currency conversion refers to the process of converting the value of one currency into the equivalent value of another currency. When dealing with foreign commerce, travel, or financial transactions involving currencies from other nations, this is frequently needed.

```r
# R
convert_currency <- function(amount, exchange_rate) {
  converted_amount <- amount * exchange_rate
  return(converted_amount)
}
# Example usage
result_r <- convert_currency(100, 1.2)
print(result_r)
```

```python
# Python
def convert_currency(amount, exchange_rate):
    converted_amount = amount * exchange_rate
    return converted_amount
# Example usage
result_py = convert_currency(100, 1.2)
print(result_py)
```

Output
R
[1] 120
Python
120.0

2. Cross Rates

Cross rates refer to the exchange rates between two currencies that do not involve the official currency of the country in which the exchange rate quote is given.

```R
# R
cross_rate <- function(rate1, rate2) {
  cross_rate_value <- rate1 / rate2
  return(cross_rate_value)
}
# Example usage
result_r <- cross_rate(1.2, 1.5)
print(result_r)
```

```python
# Python
def cross_rate(rate1, rate2):
    cross_rate_value = rate1 / rate2
    return cross_rate_value
# Example usage
result_py = cross_rate(1.2, 1.5)
print(result_py)
```

Output
R
[1] 0.8
Python
0.79

3. Forward Exchange Rate

The forward exchange rate is the exchange rate at which two parties agree to exchange currencies at a future date.

```R
# R
forward_rate <- function(spot_rate, domestic_interest, foreign_interest, time) {
  forward_rate_value <- spot_rate * (1 + domestic_interest) / (1 + foreign_interest)^(time)
  return(forward_rate_value)
}
```

```r
# Example usage
result_r <- forward_rate(1.2, 0.03, 0.02, 2)
print(result_r)
```

```python
# Python
def forward_rate(spot_rate, domestic_interest, foreign_interest, time):
    forward_rate_value = spot_rate * (1 + domestic_interest) / (1 +
foreign_interest)**(time)
    return forward_rate_value
# Example usage
result_py = forward_rate(1.2, 0.03, 0.02, 2)
print(result_py)
```

Output
R
[1] 1.188005
Python
1.1880046136101499

4. Forward Points

Forward points, also known as swap points, represent the interest rate differential between two currencies in the foreign exchange market.

```r
# R
forward_points <- function(forward_rate, spot_rate) {
 forward_points_value <- (forward_rate - spot_rate) * 10000
 return(forward_points_value)
}
# Example usage
result_r <- forward_points(1.25, 1.2)
print(result_r)
```

```python
# Python
def forward_points(forward_rate, spot_rate):
    forward_points_value = (forward_rate - spot_rate) * 10000
    return forward_points_value
# Example usage
result_py = forward_points(1.25, 1.2)
print(result_py)
```

Output
R
[1] 500
Python
500.00000000000045

5. FX Swap Points

FX point represents the interest rate differential between two currencies in a foreign exchange (forex) swap. An FX swap is a simultaneous purchase and sale of identical amounts of one currency for another with two different value dates: a near date (spot) and a future date.

```r
# R
swap_points <- function(domestic_interest, foreign_interest, time) {
  swap_points_value <- (domestic_interest - foreign_interest) * time *
10000
  return(swap_points_value)
}
# Example usage
result_r <- swap_points(0.03, 0.02, 2)
print(result_r)
```

```python
# Python
def swap_points(domestic_interest, foreign_interest, time):
    swap_points_value = (domestic_interest - foreign_interest) * time *
10000
    return swap_points_value
# Example usage
result_py = swap_points(0.03, 0.02, 2)
print(result_py)
```

Output
R
[1] 200
Python
199.99999999999997

6. Percentage Change in Exchange Rate

This represents the percentage difference between the initial exchange rate and the final exchange rate over a specific period.

```
# R
percentage_change <- function(initial_rate, final_rate) {
  percentage_change_value <- ((final_rate - initial_rate) / initial_rate) * 100
  return(percentage_change_value)
}
# Example usage
result_r <- percentage_change(50, 75)
print(result_r)
```

```
# Python
def percentage_change(initial_rate, final_rate):
    percentage_change_value = ((final_rate - initial_rate) / initial_rate) * 100
    return percentage_change_value
# Example usage
result_py = percentage_change(50, 75)
print(result_py)
```

Output
R
[1] 50
Python
50.0

7. FX Forward Rate Agreement (FRA)

FRA is a financial contract between two parties that allows them to lock in an exchange rate for a future date. It is a forward contract specifically designed to hedge against fluctuations in currency exchange rates.

```
# R
fra_rate <- function(forward_rate, spot_rate, time) {
  fra_rate_value <- (forward_rate - spot_rate) / spot_rate / (time / 365)
  return(fra_rate_value)
```

```
}
# Example usage
result_r <- fra_rate(0.045, 0.04, 90)
print(result_r)

# Python
def fra_rate(forward_rate, spot_rate, time):
    fra_rate_value = (forward_rate - spot_rate) / spot_rate / (time / 365)
    return fra_rate_value
# Example usage
result_py = fra_rate(0.045, 0.04, 90)
print(result_py)
```

Output
R
[1] 0.5069444
Python
0.50694444444

8. FX Option Premium (Black-Scholes)

The premium of an FX option is the price paid by the option buyer to the option seller for the right, but not the obligation, to buy (call option) or sell (put option) a specified amount of a currency pair at a predetermined exchange rate (strike price) on or before the option's expiration date.

```
R
library(RQuantLib)
option_premium <- function(spot_rate, strike_price, time,
domestic_interest, foreign_interest, volatility, option_type) {
  if (option_type == 'call') {
    option_premium_value <- EuropeanOption(type = option_type,
underlying = spot_rate, strike = strike_price,
dividendYield = foreign_interest, riskFreeRate = domestic_interest,
maturity = time / 365, volatility = volatility)
  } else {
    stop("Invalid option type. Choose 'call'.")
  }
  return(option_premium_value)
}
```

```
# Example for European Call Option
spot_rate <- 100
strike_price <- 100
time <- 30
domestic_interest <- 0.05
foreign_interest <- 0.02
volatility <- 0.3
option_type <- 'call'
result <- option_premium(spot_rate, strike_price, time,
domestic_interest, foreign_interest, volatility, option_type)
print(result)
```

Python Example for European Call Option:

```
from mibian import BS
def option_premium(spot_rate, strike_price, time, domestic_interest,
foreign_interest, volatility, option_type):
  if option_type == 'call':
    cp = 'c'
  else:
    raise ValueError("Invalid option type. Choose 'call'.")
  result_py = BS([spot_rate, strike_price, foreign_interest, time / 365],
          volatility=volatility * 100, callPrice=None, putPrice=None)
  option_premium_value = result_py.callPrice
  return option_premium_value


# Example
spot_rate = 100
strike_price = 100
time = 30
domestic_interest = 0.05
foreign_interest = 0.02
volatility = 0.3
option_type = 'call'
result_py = option_premium(spot_rate, strike_price, time,
domestic_interest, foreign_interest, volatility, option_type)
print(result_py)
```

Output

R

Short summary of valuation for European Option

value	delta	gamma	vega	theta	rho	divRho
3.5699	0.5279	0.0459	11.4674	-22.0465	4.1016	-4.3990

Python 0.17959909842536348

9. FX Option Delta (Black-Scholes)

Option delta is a measure that represents the sensitivity of the option's price to changes in the price of the underlying asset. It quantifies how much the option price is expected to change for a one-point change in the price of the underlying asset.

```r
# R
option_delta <- function(spot_rate, strike_price, time, domestic_interest, foreign_interest, volatility, option_type) {
  d1 <- (log(spot_rate / strike_price) + (domestic_interest - foreign_interest + 0.5 * volatility^2) * time) / (volatility * sqrt(time))
  if (option_type == "call") {
   option_delta_value <- pnorm(d1)
  } else if (option_type == "put") {
   option_delta_value <- pnorm(d1) - 1
  }
  return(option_delta_value)
}
```

```r
# Example usage
spot_rate_example <- 50
strike_price_example <- 45
time_example <- 0.5
domestic_interest_example <- 0.05
foreign_interest_example <- 0.03
volatility_example <- 0.25
option_type_example <- "call"
option_delta(spot_rate_example, strike_price_example, time_example, domestic_interest_example, foreign_interest_example, volatility_example, option_type_example)
```

Python Example:

```python
# Python
import math
from scipy.stats import norm
def option_delta(spot_rate, strike_price, time, domestic_interest, foreign_interest, volatility, option_type):
```

```
    d1 = (math.log(spot_rate / strike_price) + (domestic_interest -
foreign_interest + 0.5 * volatility ** 2) * time) / (volatility *
math.sqrt(time))
    if option_type == 'call':
        option_delta_value = norm.cdf(d1)
    elif option_type == 'put':
        option_delta_value = norm.cdf(d1) - 1
    return option_delta_value

# Example usage
spot_rate_example = 50
strike_price_example = 45
time_example = 0.5
domestic_interest_example = 0.05
foreign_interest_example = 0.03
volatility_example = 0.25
option_type_example = "call"
print(option_delta(spot_rate_example,            strike_price_example,
time_example, domestic_interest_example, foreign_interest_example,
volatility_example, option_type_example))
```

Output
```
R
[1] 0.770643
Python
0.7706429632810612
```

10. FX Option Vega (Black-Scholes)

Option Vega is the sensitivity of an option's price to changes in volatility.
It quantifies how much the option price is expected to change for a 1%
change in the volatility of the underlying asset's returns.

```
# R
library(stats)
option_vega <- function(spot_rate, strike_price, time, domestic_interest,
foreign_interest, volatility) {
    d1 <- (log(spot_rate / strike_price) + (domestic_interest -
foreign_interest + 0.5 * volatility^2) * time) / (volatility * sqrt(time))
    option_vega_value <- spot_rate * sqrt(time) * dnorm(d1)
    return(option_vega_value)
}
```

```
# Example usage
spot_rate_example <- 50
strike_price_example <- 45
time_example <- 0.5
domestic_interest_example <- 0.05
foreign_interest_example <- 0.03
volatility_example <- 0.25
option_vega(spot_rate_example, strike_price_example, time_example,
domestic_interest_example, foreign_interest_example,
volatility_example)
```

```python
# Python
import math
from scipy.stats import norm
def option_vega(spot_rate, strike_price, time, domestic_interest,
foreign_interest, volatility):
    d1 = (math.log(spot_rate / strike_price) + (domestic_interest -
foreign_interest + 0.5 * volatility ** 2) * time) / (volatility *
math.sqrt(time))
    option_vega_value = spot_rate * math.sqrt(time) * norm.pdf(d1)
    return option_vega_value
```

```python
# Example usage
spot_rate_example = 50
strike_price_example = 45
time_example = 0.5
domestic_interest_example = 0.05
foreign_interest_example = 0.03
volatility_example = 0.25
print(option_vega(spot_rate_example, strike_price_example,
time_example, domestic_interest_example, foreign_interest_example,
volatility_example))
```

Output
R
[1] 10.71876
Python
10.718761282379333

11. FX Option Theta (Black-Scholes)

Option Theta measures the sensitivity of an option's price to the passage of time. It quantifies how much the option price is expected to change for a one-day decrease in the time to expiration.

```r
# R
option_theta <- function(spot_rate, strike_price, time, domestic_interest,
foreign_interest, volatility) {
  d1 <- (log(spot_rate / strike_price) + (domestic_interest -
foreign_interest + 0.5 * volatility^2) * time) / (volatility * sqrt(time))
  d2 <- d1 - volatility * sqrt(time)
  option_theta_value <- -spot_rate * dnorm(d1) * volatility / (2 *
sqrt(time)) - (domestic_interest - foreign_interest) * strike_price * exp(-
domestic_interest * time) * pnorm(d2)
  return(option_theta_value)
}
# Example usage in R
spot_rate_example <- 50
strike_price_example <- 45
time_example <- 0.5
domestic_interest_example <- 0.05
foreign_interest_example <- 0.03
volatility_example <- 0.25
option_theta(spot_rate_example, strike_price_example, time_example,
domestic_interest_example,                     foreign_interest_example,
volatility_example)
```

```python
from scipy.stats import norm
import math
def option_theta(spot_rate, strike_price, time, domestic_interest,
foreign_interest, volatility):
    d1 = (math.log(spot_rate / strike_price) + (domestic_interest -
foreign_interest + 0.5 * volatility ** 2) * time) / (volatility *
math.sqrt(time))
    d2 = d1 - volatility * math.sqrt(time)
    option_theta_value = -spot_rate * norm.pdf(d1) * volatility / (2 *
math.sqrt(time)) - (domestic_interest - foreign_interest) * strike_price *
math.exp(-domestic_interest * time) * norm.cdf(d2)
    return option_theta_value


# Example usage in Python
spot_rate_example = 50
```

```
strike_price_example = 45
time_example = 0.5
domestic_interest_example = 0.05
foreign_interest_example = 0.03
volatility_example = 0.25
result    =    option_theta(spot_rate_example,   strike_price_example,
time_example,  domestic_interest_example,  foreign_interest_example,
volatility_example)
print(result)
```

Output
R
[1] -3.30615
Python
-3.306150021230838

12. FX Option Gamma (Black-Scholes)

Option Gamma measures the rate of change of an option's delta with
respect to changes in the price of the underlying asset. It quantifies how
much the option delta is expected to change for a one-point change in the
price of the underlying asset.

```
# R
option_gamma    <-    function(spot_rate,    strike_price,    time,
domestic_interest, foreign_interest, volatility) {
 d1   <-   (log(spot_rate  /  strike_price)  +  (domestic_interest  -
foreign_interest + 0.5 * volatility^2) * time) / (volatility * sqrt(time))
 option_gamma_value <- dnorm(d1) / (spot_rate * volatility * sqrt(time))
 return(option_gamma_value)
}
# Example usage in R
spot_rate_example <- 50
strike_price_example <- 45
time_example <- 0.5
domestic_interest_example <- 0.05
foreign_interest_example <- 0.03
volatility_example <- 0.25
result <- option_gamma(spot_rate_example, strike_price_example,
time_example, domestic_interest_example, foreign_interest_example,
volatility_example)
print(result)
```

```python
# Python
import math
from scipy.stats import norm
def option_gamma(spot_rate, strike_price, time, domestic_interest,
foreign_interest, volatility):
    d1 = (math.log(spot_rate / strike_price) + (domestic_interest -
foreign_interest + 0.5 * volatility ** 2) * time) / (volatility *
math.sqrt(time))
    option_gamma_value = norm.pdf(d1) / (spot_rate * volatility *
math.sqrt(time))
    return option_gamma_value
# Example usage in Python
spot_rate_example = 50
strike_price_example = 45
time_example = 0.5
domestic_interest_example = 0.05
foreign_interest_example = 0.03
volatility_example = 0.25
result = option_gamma(spot_rate_example, strike_price_example,
time_example, domestic_interest_example, foreign_interest_example,
volatility_example)
print(result)
```

Output
R
[1] 0.03430004
Python
0.034300036103613867

13. FX Option Rho (Black-Scholes)

Option Rho measures the sensitivity of an option's price to changes in the risk-free interest rate. It quantifies how much the option price is expected to change for a one-percentage-point change in the risk-free interest rate.

```r
# R
option_rho <- function(spot_rate, strike_price, time, domestic_interest,
foreign_interest, volatility, option_type) {
  d2 <- (log(spot_rate / strike_price) + (domestic_interest -
foreign_interest - 0.5 * volatility^2) * time) / (volatility * sqrt(time))
  if (option_type == "call") {
```

```r
   option_rho_value <- strike_price * time * exp(-domestic_interest *
time) * pnorm(d2)
  } else if (option_type == "put") {
   option_rho_value <- -strike_price * time * exp(-domestic_interest *
time) * pnorm(-d2)
  }
 return(option_rho_value)
}

# Example usage in R
spot_rate_example <- 50
strike_price_example <- 45
time_example <- 0.5
domestic_interest_example <- 0.05
foreign_interest_example <- 0.03
volatility_example <- 0.25
option_type_example <- "call"
result <- option_rho(spot_rate_example, strike_price_example,
time_example, domestic_interest_example, foreign_interest_example,
volatility_example, option_type_example)
print(result)
```

```python
# Python
import math
from scipy.stats import norm
def  option_rho(spot_rate,  strike_price,  time,  domestic_interest,
foreign_interest, volatility, option_type):
    d2  =  (math.log(spot_rate  /  strike_price)  +  (domestic_interest  -
foreign_interest - 0.5 * volatility ** 2) * time) / (volatility *
math.sqrt(time))
    if option_type == 'call':
        option_rho_value  =  strike_price  *  time  *  math.exp(-
domestic_interest * time) * norm.cdf(d2)
    elif option_type == 'put':
        option_rho_value  =  -strike_price  *  time  *  math.exp(-
domestic_interest * time) * norm.cdf(-d2)
    return option_rho_value
# Example usage in Python
spot_rate_example = 50
strike_price_example = 45
time_example = 0.5
domestic_interest_example = 0.05
```

```r
foreign_interest_example = 0.03
volatility_example = 0.25
option_type_example = 'call'
result   =   option_rho(spot_rate_example,   strike_price_example,
time_example, domestic_interest_example, foreign_interest_example,
volatility_example, option_type_example)
print(result)
```

Output
R
[1] 15.66149
Python
15.661492515900136

14. FX Option Implied Volatility (Black-Scholes)

Option Implied Volatility is the volatility value that, when input into the
Black-Scholes formula, yields the observed market price of the option. It
is the market's expectation of future volatility as implied by the current
option prices.

R
```r
# Define parameters
spot <- 1.20  # Spot exchange rate
strike <- 1.25  # Strike price
call_price <- 0.05  # Call option price
risk_free_rate <- 0.05  # Risk-free rate
time_to_maturity <- 0.5  # Time to maturity in years
sigma <- 0.20  # Implied volatility (initial guess)
# Define the Black-Scholes call price function
black_scholes_call <- function(sigma) {
  d1 <- (log(spot / strike) + (risk_free_rate + 0.5 * sigma^2) *
time_to_maturity) / (sigma * sqrt(time_to_maturity))
  d2 <- d1 - sigma * sqrt(time_to_maturity)
  call_price_theoretical <- spot * pnorm(d1) - strike * exp(-risk_free_rate
* time_to_maturity) * pnorm(d2)
  return(call_price_theoretical - call_price)
}
# Use the uniroot function to find the implied volatility
implied_volatility <- uniroot(black_scholes_call, interval = c(0.01, 1.0))
# Print implied volatility
print(implied_volatility)
```

```python
#Python
pip install numpy scipy
from scipy.optimize import root_scalar
from scipy.stats import norm
import numpy as np
# Define parameters
spot = 1.20  # Spot exchange rate
strike = 1.25  # Strike price
call_price = 0.05  # Call option price
risk_free_rate = 0.05  # Risk-free rate
time_to_maturity = 0.5  # Time to maturity in years
sigma_guess = 0.20  # Implied volatility (initial guess)
# Define the Black-Scholes call price function
def black_scholes_call(sigma):
    d1 = (np.log(spot / strike) + (risk_free_rate + 0.5 * sigma**2) *
time_to_maturity) / (sigma * np.sqrt(time_to_maturity))
    d2 = d1 - sigma * np.sqrt(time_to_maturity)
    call_price_theoretical = spot * norm.cdf(d1) - strike * np.exp(-
risk_free_rate * time_to_maturity) * norm.cdf(d2)
    return call_price_theoretical - call_price
# Use the root_scalar function to find the implied volatility
result = root_scalar(black_scholes_call, bracket=[0.01, 1.0])
implied_volatility = result.root
# Print implied volatility
print(f"Implied Volatility: {implied_volatility:.4f}")
```

Output
R
$root [1] 0.1732468
$f.root [1] -1.571775e-07
$iter [1] 4
$init.it [1] NA
$estim.prec [1] 6.103516e-05
Python
Implied Volatility: 0.1732

15. FX Option Risk Reversal and Butterflies

The butterfly spread aims to capitalize on low volatility in the underlying asset. A risk reversal is an options trading strategy that combines buying and selling different types of options to create a position that profits from

172

changes in the price of the underlying asset. A butterfly spread is an options trading strategy that involves using three strike prices to create a position with limited risk and limited profit potential.

```r
# R example
call_delta <- 0.6
put_delta <- 0.4
risk_reversal <- call_delta - put_delta
butterfly <- (call_delta + put_delta) / 2
print(paste("Risk Reversal Value:", risk_reversal))
print(paste("Butterfly Value:", butterfly))
```

```python
# Python example
call_delta = 0.6
put_delta = 0.4
risk_reversal = call_delta - put_delta
butterfly = (call_delta + put_delta) / 2
print("Risk Reversal Value:", risk_reversal)
print("Butterfly Value:", butterfly)
```

Output
R
[1] "Risk Reversal Value: 0.2"
[1] "Butterfly Value: 0.5"
Python
Risk Reversal Value: 0.19999999999999996
Butterfly Value: 0.5

The value of a butterfly spread in options trading is the difference between the option premiums paid and received when establishing the position. The value of the risk reversal is the net cost or credit of the options involved, depending on whether the call option is more expensive than the put option or vice versa.

16. FX Option Strike from Delta (Black-Scholes)

Delta is used to represent the sensitivity of an option's price to changes in the price of the underlying asset. It refers to the process of determining the strike price of an option based on a desired delta.

```r
# R example
strike_from_delta <- function(spot_rate, time, domestic_interest,
foreign_interest, volatility, delta, option_type) {
 d1 <- qnorm(delta) + (volatility * sqrt(time)) / 2
 if (option_type == "call") {
  strike_from_delta_value <- spot_rate * exp((foreign_interest -
domestic_interest) * time) * pnorm(d1)
 } else if (option_type == "put") {
  strike_from_delta_value <- spot_rate * exp((foreign_interest -
domestic_interest) * time) * pnorm(d1) - (pnorm(d1) - 1) * spot_rate
 }
 return(strike_from_delta_value)
}
# Example data
spot_rate <- 1.2
time <- 0.5
domestic_interest <- 0.03
foreign_interest <- 0.02
volatility <- 0.2
delta <- 0.6
option_type <- "call"
result <- strike_from_delta(spot_rate, time, domestic_interest,
foreign_interest, volatility, delta, option_type)
print(result)

# Python
from scipy.stats import norm
def strike_from_delta(spot_rate, time, domestic_interest,
foreign_interest, volatility, delta, option_type):
  d1 = norm.ppf(delta) + (volatility * (time ** 0.5)) / 2
  if option_type == "call":
    strike_from_delta_value = spot_rate * (foreign_interest * time) *
norm.cdf(d1)
  elif option_type == "put":
    strike_from_delta_value = spot_rate * (foreign_interest * time) *
norm.cdf(d1) - (norm.cdf(d1) - 1) * spot_rate
  return strike_from_delta_value
# Usage
spot_rate = 1.2
time = 0.5
domestic_interest = 0.03
foreign_interest = 0.02
```

```
volatility = 0.2
delta = 0.6
option_type = "call"
result = strike_from_delta(spot_rate, time, domestic_interest,
foreign_interest, volatility, delta, option_type)
print(result)
```

Output
R
[1] 0.7487105
Python
0.0075246342641871414

17. FX Option Payoff

Option Payoff is the profit or loss that an investor realizes from holding a
foreign exchange option position at expiration. The payoff depends on the
spot exchange rate at the time of expiration and the terms of the option
contract.

```
# R example
option_payoff <- function(spot_rate, strike_price, option_type) {
  if (option_type == "call") {
    option_payoff_value <- ifelse(spot_rate > strike_price, spot_rate -
strike_price, 0)
  } else if (option_type == "put") {
    option_payoff_value <- ifelse(spot_rate < strike_price, strike_price -
spot_rate, 0)
  }
  return(option_payoff_value)
}
# Usage
spot_rate <- 1.2
strike_price <- 1.3
option_type <- "call"
result <- option_payoff(spot_rate, strike_price, option_type)
print(result)

# Python example
def option_payoff(spot_rate, strike_price, option_type):
  if option_type == "call":
    option_payoff_value = max(0, spot_rate - strike_price)
```

```
  elif option_type == "put":
    option_payoff_value = max(0, strike_price - spot_rate)
  return option_payoff_value
# Usage
spot_rate = 1.2
strike_price = 1.3
option_type = "call"
result = option_payoff(spot_rate, strike_price, option_type)
print(result)
```

Output
R [1] 0, Python 0

18. FX Option Break-Even Rates

Option Break-Even Rates refer to the spot exchange rates at which the payoff from holding an FX option position becomes zero. It is the level at which the gains from the option offset the initial premium paid for the option, resulting in neither a profit nor a loss.

```
# R
# Define function
option_breakeven <- function(spot_rate, call_premium, put_premium,
option_type) {
  if (option_type == "call") {
  option_breakeven_value <- spot_rate + call_premium
  } else if (option_type == "put") {
  option_breakeven_value <- spot_rate - put_premium
  }
  return(option_breakeven_value)
}
# Example usage
spot_rate <- 100  # Replace with your actual spot rate
call_premium <- 5 # Replace with your actual call premium
put_premium <- 3  # Replace with your actual put premium
option_type <- "call"  # Replace with "put" for put option
# Calculate breakeven value
breakeven_value <- option_breakeven(spot_rate, call_premium,
put_premium, option_type)
# Print the result
print(paste("Breakeven Value:", breakeven_value))
```

```python
# Python
def option_breakeven(spot_rate, call_premium, put_premium,
option_type):
    if option_type == 'call':
        option_breakeven_value = spot_rate + call_premium
    elif option_type == 'put':
        option_breakeven_value = spot_rate - put_premium
    return option_breakeven_value
# Example usage
spot_rate = 100  # Replace with your actual spot rate
call_premium = 5  # Replace with your actual call premium
put_premium = 3  # Replace with your actual put premium
option_type = 'call'  # Replace with 'put' for put option
# Calculate breakeven value
breakeven_value = option_breakeven(spot_rate, call_premium,
put_premium, option_type)
# Print the result
print(f"Breakeven Value: {breakeven_value}")
```

Output
R
[1] "Breakeven Value: 105"
Python
Breakeven Value: 105

19. FX Option Spread

Option Spread involves the simultaneous purchase and sale of multiple options on the same underlying currency pair. Option spreads are constructed with the aim of capitalizing on price movements, volatility expectations, or other market conditions.

R:
```r
calculate_break_even <- function(spot_rate, premium, call_strike,
put_strike) {
  call_break_even <- call_strike + premium
  put_break_even <- put_strike - premium

  return(list(call_break_even = call_break_even, put_break_even =
put_break_even))
}
```

```
# Example usage
spot_rate <- 1.2
premium <- 0.02
call_strike <- 1.25
put_strike <- 1.15
break_even <- calculate_break_even(spot_rate, premium, call_strike,
put_strike)
print(break_even)
```

Python:
```
def calculate_break_even(spot_rate, premium, call_strike, put_strike):
    call_break_even = call_strike + premium
    put_break_even = put_strike - premium
    return call_break_even, put_break_even
# Example usage
spot_rate = 1.2
premium = 0.02
call_strike = 1.25
put_strike = 1.15
break_even = calculate_break_even(spot_rate, premium, call_strike,
put_strike)
print(break_even)
```

Output
R
Call_break_even
[1] 1.27
Put_break_even
[1] 1.13
Python
(1.27, 1.13)

20. FX Option Hedge Ratios (Delta Hedging)

Option Hedge Ratios are measures used by traders to determine the amount of the underlying currency (spot position) that needs to be bought or sold to offset the risk associated with holding a specific option position.

R:
```
calculate_hedge_ratio <- function(call_delta, put_delta) {
  call_hedge_ratio <- call_delta
  put_hedge_ratio <- put_delta
```

```r
  return(list(call_hedge_ratio  =  call_hedge_ratio,  put_hedge_ratio  =
put_hedge_ratio))
}
# Example usage
call_delta <- 0.7
put_delta <- -0.3
hedge_ratios <- calculate_hedge_ratio(call_delta, put_delta)
print(hedge_ratios)
```

Python:
```python
def calculate_hedge_ratio(call_delta, put_delta):
    call_hedge_ratio = call_delta
    put_hedge_ratio = put_delta
    return call_hedge_ratio, put_hedge_ratio
# Example usage
call_delta = 0.7
put_delta = -0.3
hedge_ratios = calculate_hedge_ratio(call_delta, put_delta)
print(hedge_ratios)
```

Output
R
Call_hedge_ratio
[1] 0.7
Put_hedge_ratio
[1] -0.3
Python
(0.7, -0.3)

CHAPTER 7

This chapter covers 20 commonly used code examples for bond calculations in both R and Python.

1. Bond Price

The Bond Price refers to the current market value or the present worth of a bond. It represents the amount an investor is willing to pay for a bond in the open market.

R:
```
calculate_bond_price <- function(coupon, ytm, face_value,
years_to_maturity) {
  bond_price <- (coupon * (1 - (1 + ytm)^-years_to_maturity) / ytm) +
(face_value / (1 + ytm)^years_to_maturity)
  return(bond_price)
}
# Example usage
coupon <- 50
ytm <- 0.05
face_value <- 1000
years_to_maturity <- 5
bond_price <- calculate_bond_price(coupon, ytm, face_value,
years_to_maturity)
print(bond_price)
```

Python:
```
def calculate_bond_price(coupon, ytm, face_value, years_to_maturity):
    bond_price = (coupon * (1 - (1 + ytm)**-years_to_maturity) / ytm) +
(face_value / (1 + ytm)**years_to_maturity)
    return bond_price
# Example usage
coupon = 50
ytm = 0.05
face_value = 1000
years_to_maturity = 5
bond_price = calculate_bond_price(coupon, ytm, face_value,
years_to_maturity)
```

```
print(bond_price)
```

Output
R
[1] 1000
Python
999.9999999999999

2. Bond YTM (Yield to Maturity)

The Yield to Maturity (YTM) of a bond is the total return anticipated on a bond if it is held until it matures. It is expressed as an annual percentage rate and considers the bond's current market price, par value, coupon interest rate, and the number of years remaining until maturity.

R:
```
# Define the function to calculate YTM
calculate_bond_ytm <- function(coupon, price, face_value,
years_to_maturity) {
  ytm_func <- function(ytm) {
    price - (coupon * (1 - (1 + ytm)^-years_to_maturity) / ytm) -
(face_value / (1 + ytm)^years_to_maturity)
  }
  ytm <- uniroot(ytm_func, interval = c(0.0001, 1), extendInt =
"yes")$root
  return(ytm)
}
# Example usage
coupon <- 50
price <- 950
face_value <- 1000
years_to_maturity <- 5
ytm <- calculate_bond_ytm(coupon, price, face_value,
years_to_maturity)
print(ytm)
```

Python:
```
from scipy.optimize import brentq
# Define the function to calculate YTM
def calculate_bond_ytm(coupon, price, face_value, years_to_maturity):
    def ytm_func(ytm):
```

```
    return price - (coupon * (1 - (1 + ytm)**-years_to_maturity) / ytm)
- (face_value / (1 + ytm)**years_to_maturity)
   ytm = brentq(ytm_func, 0.0001, 1)
   return ytm
# Example usage
coupon = 50
price = 950
face_value = 1000
years_to_maturity = 5
ytm = calculate_bond_ytm(coupon, price, face_value,
years_to_maturity)
print(ytm)
```

Output
R
[1] 0.06193394
Python
0.061932282681517216

3. Bond Accrued Interest

Bond Accrued Interest refers to the interest that has accumulated on a bond since its last interest payment date. When a bond pays periodic interest, typically semiannually or annually, the interest is calculated based on the bond's coupon rate and face value.

R:
```
# Define the function to calculate bond accrued interest
calculate_accrued_interest <- function(coupon,
days_since_last_payment, days_in_period) {
  accrued_interest <- (coupon / days_in_period) *
days_since_last_payment
  return(accrued_interest)
}
# Example usage
coupon <- 50
days_since_last_payment <- 30
days_in_period <- 180
accrued_interest <- calculate_accrued_interest(coupon,
days_since_last_payment, days_in_period)
print(accrued_interest)
```

Python:
```python
# Define the function to calculate bond accrued interest
def calculate_accrued_interest(coupon, days_since_last_payment,
days_in_period):
    accrued_interest = (coupon / days_in_period) *
days_since_last_payment
    return accrued_interest
# Example usage
coupon = 50
days_since_last_payment = 30
days_in_period = 180
accrued_interest = calculate_accrued_interest(coupon,
days_since_last_payment, days_in_period)
print(accrued_interest)
```

Output
R
[1] 8.333333
Python
8.333333333333334

4. Current Yield of a Bond

The Current Yield of a bond is a measure of its annual interest income relative to its current market price. It is expressed as a percentage and provides investors with a quick way to assess the income generated by a bond investment.

R:
```r
# Define the function to calculate current yield
calculate_current_yield <- function(coupon, price) {
  current_yield <- (coupon / price) * 100
  return(current_yield)
}
# Example usage
coupon <- 50
price <- 950
current_yield <- calculate_current_yield(coupon, price)
print(current_yield)
```

Python:
```python
# Define the function to calculate current yield
```

```
def calculate_current_yield(coupon, price):
    current_yield = (coupon / price) * 100
    return current_yield
# Example usage
coupon = 50
price = 950
current_yield = calculate_current_yield(coupon, price)
print(current_yield)
```

Output
R
[1] 5.263158
Python
5.263157894736842

5. Macaulay Duration of a Bond

Macaulay Duration is a measure of the weighted average time it takes for the present value of a bond's cash flows to repay its initial price. It is used to estimate the interest rate risk of a bond, providing insight into how sensitive the bond's price is to changes in interest rates.

```
# R
# Define the function
macaulay_duration <- function(coupon_rate, face_value,
yield_to_maturity, time_to_maturity) {
  macaulay_duration_value <- (time_to_maturity * (1 +
yield_to_maturity)) / ((1 + yield_to_maturity) ^ time_to_maturity) *
(coupon_rate / yield_to_maturity) + time_to_maturity
  return(macaulay_duration_value)
}
# Example values
coupon_rate <- 0.05  # 5% coupon rate
face_value <- 1000   # Face value of the bond
yield_to_maturity <- 0.03  # 3% yield to maturity
time_to_maturity <- 5  # 5 years to maturity
# Calculate Macaulay duration
duration_value <- macaulay_duration(coupon_rate, face_value,
yield_to_maturity, time_to_maturity)
# Print the result
cat("Macaulay Duration:", duration_value, "\n")
```

```python
# Python
def macaulay_duration(coupon_rate, face_value, yield_to_maturity,
time_to_maturity):
    macaulay_duration_value = (time_to_maturity * (1 +
yield_to_maturity)) / ((1 + yield_to_maturity) ** time_to_maturity) *
(coupon_rate / yield_to_maturity) + time_to_maturity
    return macaulay_duration_value
# Example values
coupon_rate = 0.05  # 5% coupon rate
face_value = 1000   # Face value of the bond
yield_to_maturity = 0.03  # 3% yield to maturity
time_to_maturity = 5  # 5 years to maturity
# Calculate Macaulay duration
duration_value = macaulay_duration(coupon_rate, face_value,
yield_to_maturity, time_to_maturity)
# Print the result
print("Macaulay Duration:", duration_value)
```

Output
R
Macaulay Duration: 12.40406
Python
Macaulay Duration: 12.404058732630741

6. Modified Duration of a Bond

Modified Duration is a measure of the sensitivity of a bond's price to changes in interest rates. It is an adjusted version of Macaulay Duration that provides a percentage change in the bond's price for a 1% change in yield.

R:
```r
# Define the function to calculate Macaulay Duration
calculate_macaulay_duration <- function(cash_flows, discount_rates,
periods) {
  weighted_sum <- sum(cash_flows * discount_rates)
  macaulay_duration <- weighted_sum / sum(cash_flows) * periods
  return(macaulay_duration)
}
# Example usage
cash_flows <- c(50, 50, 50, 1050)
discount_rates <- c(0.05, 0.05, 0.05, 0.05)
```

```r
periods <- 4
macaulay_duration <- calculate_macaulay_duration(cash_flows,
discount_rates, periods)
print(macaulay_duration)
```

Python:
```python
# Define the function to calculate Macaulay Duration
def calculate_macaulay_duration(cash_flows, discount_rates, periods):
    weighted_sum = sum(cash_flows * discount_rates)
    macaulay_duration = weighted_sum / sum(cash_flows) * periods
    return macaulay_duration
# Example usage
cash_flows = [50, 50, 50, 1050]
discount_rates = [0.05, 0.05, 0.05, 0.05]
periods = 4
macaulay_duration = calculate_macaulay_duration(cash_flows,
discount_rates, periods)
print(macaulay_duration)
```

Output
R
[1] 0.2
Python
0.2

7. Convexity of a Bond

Convexity is a measure of the curvature or the second-order sensitivity of a bond's price to changes in interest rates. While duration provides a linear approximation of a bond's price change in response to interest rate movements, convexity takes into account the curvature of the price-yield curve.

```r
# R
calculate_convexity <- function(cash_flows, discount_rates, periods,
ytm) {
  cash_flows <- as.numeric(cash_flows)
  discount_rates <- as.numeric(discount_rates)
  periods <- as.numeric(periods)
  ytm <- as.numeric(ytm)
  present_value <- sum(cash_flows / (1 + ytm) ^ periods)
```

```r
  convexity <- sum(cash_flows * periods * (periods + 1) / (1 + ytm) ^
(periods + 2)) / present_value
  return(convexity)
}
# Example usage
cash_flows <- c(50, 50, 50, 1050)
discount_rates <- c(0.05, 0.05, 0.05, 0.05)
periods <- 1:4
ytm <- 0.05
convexity <- calculate_convexity(cash_flows, discount_rates, periods,
ytm)
convexity
```

```python
# Python
import numpy as np
def calculate_convexity(cash_flows, discount_rates, periods, ytm):
    cash_flows = np.array(cash_flows)
    discount_rates = np.array(discount_rates)
    periods = np.array(periods)
    ytm = np.array(ytm)
    present_value = np.sum(cash_flows / (1 + ytm) ** periods)
    convexity = np.sum(cash_flows * periods * (periods + 1) / (1 + ytm) **
(periods + 2)) / present_value
    return convexity
# Example usage
cash_flows = [50, 50, 50, 1050]
discount_rates = [0.05, 0.05, 0.05, 0.05]
periods = np.array([1, 2, 3, 4])
ytm = 0.05
convexity = calculate_convexity(cash_flows, discount_rates, periods,
ytm)
convexity
print(convexity)
```

Output
R
[1] 16.47383
Python
16.47383353154097

8. Bond Duration and Convexity for Parallel Yield Shift

For a parallel yield shift, where all interest rates across the yield curve change by the same amount, the concepts of bond duration and convexity play a crucial role in understanding how the bond's price would respond. If there is a parallel increase (or decrease) in interest rates across the yield curve, the impact on bond prices can be estimated using duration and convexity.

```r
# R
calculate_duration_convexity <- function(cash_flows, discount_rates,
ytm_change) {
  present_value <- sum(cash_flows / (1 + discount_rates)^2)
  duration <- -sum(cash_flows * discount_rates / (1 + discount_rates)) /
present_value
  convexity <- sum(cash_flows * (1 + discount_rates)^2 / present_value)
- 1
  new_present_value <- sum(cash_flows / (1 + (discount_rates +
ytm_change))^2)
  new_duration <- -sum(cash_flows * (discount_rates + ytm_change) / (1
+ (discount_rates + ytm_change))) / new_present_value
  new_convexity <- sum(cash_flows * (1 + (discount_rates +
ytm_change))^2 / new_present_value) - 1
  return(list(duration = duration, convexity = convexity, new_duration =
new_duration, new_convexity = new_convexity))
}
# Example usage
cash_flows <- c(50, 50, 50, 1050)
discount_rates <- c(0.05, 0.05, 0.05, 0.05)
ytm_change <- 0.01
calculate_duration_convexity(cash_flows, discount_rates, ytm_change)
```

```python
# Python
import numpy as np
def calculate_duration_convexity(cash_flows, discount_rates,
ytm_change):
    cash_flows = np.array(cash_flows)
    discount_rates = np.array(discount_rates)
    present_value = np.sum(cash_flows / (1 + discount_rates) ** 2)
    duration = -np.sum(cash_flows * discount_rates / (1 +
discount_rates)) / present_value
```

```python
    convexity = np.sum(cash_flows * (1 + discount_rates) ** 2 /
present_value) - 1
    new_present_value = np.sum(cash_flows / (1 + (discount_rates +
ytm_change)) ** 2)
    new_duration = -np.sum(cash_flows * (discount_rates + ytm_change)
/ (1 + (discount_rates + ytm_change))) / new_present_value
    new_convexity = np.sum(cash_flows * (1 + (discount_rates +
ytm_change)) ** 2 / new_present_value) - 1
    return {
        "duration": duration,
        "convexity": convexity,
        "new_duration": new_duration,
        "new_convexity": new_convexity
    }
# Example usage
cash_flows = [50, 50, 50, 1050]
discount_rates = [0.05, 0.05, 0.05, 0.05]
ytm_change = 0.01
print(calculate_duration_convexity(cash_flows, discount_rates,
ytm_change))
```

Output
R
$duration
[1] -0.0525
$convexity
[1] 0.2155063
$new_duration
[1] -0.0636
$new_convexity
[1] 0.262477

Python
{'duration': -0.0525, 'convexity': 0.21550625000000023, 'new_duration':
-0.0636, 'new_convexity': 0.2624769600000003}

9. Bond Yield Based on Cash Flows

The bond yield based on cash flows refers to the calculation of the yield
of a bond by considering its future cash flows, including both interest
payments and the return of principal at maturity.

189

```r
# R
calculate_yield <- function(cash_flows, price) {
  ytm_func <- function(rate, cash_flows, price) sum(cash_flows / (1 +
rate)^(1:length(cash_flows))) - price
  yield <- uniroot(ytm_func, interval = c(-0.99, 0.99), cash_flows =
cash_flows, price = price)$root * 100
  return(yield)
}
# Example usage
cash_flows <- c(-1000, 100, 100, 100, 100, 1100)
price <- 1000
calculate_yield(cash_flows, price)
print(cash_flows)
```

```python
# Python
from scipy.optimize import newton
import numpy as np
def calculate_yield(cash_flows, price):
    cash_flows = np.array(cash_flows)
    def ytm_func(rate):
        return np.sum(cash_flows / (1 + rate) ** np.arange(1,
len(cash_flows) + 1)) - price
    rate = newton(ytm_func, x0=0)
    yield_value = rate * 100
    return yield_value
# Example usage
cash_flows = [-1000, 100, 100, 100, 100, 1100]
price = 1000
print(calculate_yield(cash_flows, price))
```

Output
R
[1] -5.73467
Python
-5.736103937909749

10. Yield to Call (YTC) for Callable Bonds

Yield to Call (YTC) is a measure of the expected yield of a callable bond, considering the possibility that the issuer may exercise its right to call (redeem) the bond before its maturity date. Callable bonds give issuers the option to redeem the bonds before the scheduled maturity, typically at a specified "call price".

```R
# R
calculate_yield_to_call <- function(coupon, price, call_price, years_to_call) {
  ytc_func <- function(rate, coupon, price, call_price, years_to_call) {
    cf <- rep(coupon, years_to_call)
    cf[length(cf)] <- cf[length(cf)] + call_price
    return(sum(cf / (1 + rate)^(1:years_to_call)) - price)
  }
  # Use uniroot function to find yield to call
  yield_to_call <- uniroot(ytc_func, c(0, 1), coupon = coupon, price = price, call_price = call_price, years_to_call = years_to_call)$root * 100
  return(yield_to_call)
}
# Example usage
coupon <- 40
price <- 1000
call_price <- 1100
years_to_call <- 5
# Calculate Yield to Call
result <- calculate_yield_to_call(coupon, price, call_price, years_to_call)
# Print the result
cat("Yield to Call:", result, "\n")
```

```python
# Python
from scipy.optimize import newton
def calculate_yield_to_call(coupon, price, call_price, years_to_call):
    def ytc_func(rate, coupon, price, call_price, years_to_call):
        cf = [coupon] * years_to_call
        cf[-1] += call_price
        return sum([cf[i] / (1 + rate) ** (i + 1) for i in range(years_to_call)]) - price
    yield_to_call = newton(ytc_func, 0, args=(coupon, price, call_price, years_to_call)) * 100
    return yield_to_call
# Example usage
coupon = 40
price = 1000
call_price = 1100
years_to_call = 5
```

```
result = calculate_yield_to_call(coupon, price, call_price, years_to_call)
print(f"Yield to Call: {result}")
```

Output
R
Yield to Call: 5.781823
Python
Yield to Call: 5.781712745771562

11. Duration for a Bond Portfolio

Duration for a bond portfolio is a measure of the average sensitivity of the portfolio's value to changes in interest rates. It quantifies the price risk associated with interest rate movements for the entire portfolio.

```r
# R
calculate_portfolio_duration <- function(weights, durations) {
  portfolio_duration <- sum(weights * durations)
  return(portfolio_duration)
}
# Example usage
weights <- c(0.4, 0.3, 0.3)
durations <- c(3, 4, 5)
result <- calculate_portfolio_duration(weights, durations)
result
```

```python
# Python
def calculate_portfolio_duration(weights, durations):
    portfolio_duration = sum([w * d for w, d in zip(weights, durations)])
    return portfolio_duration
# Example usage
weights = [0.4, 0.3, 0.3]
durations = [3, 4, 5]
result – calculate_portfolio_duration(weights, durations)
print(result)
```

Output
R
[1] 3.9
Python
3.9000000000000004
```
```

12. Modified Duration for a Bond Portfolio

Modified Duration for a bond portfolio is a measure of the sensitivity of the portfolio's value to changes in interest rates, adjusted for the bond's yield. It is a modified or adjusted version of Macaulay Duration, taking into account the fact that interest rate changes can also impact the bond's yield.

```r
# R
calculate_portfolio_modified_duration <- function(weights,
modified_durations) {
  portfolio_modified_duration <- sum(weights * modified_durations)
  return(portfolio_modified_duration)
}
# Example usage
weights <- c(0.4, 0.3, 0.3)
modified_durations <- c(2.5, 3.8, 4.2)
result <- calculate_portfolio_modified_duration(weights,
modified_durations)
result
```

```python
# Python
def calculate_portfolio_modified_duration(weights,
modified_durations):
    portfolio_modified_duration = sum([w * d for w, d in zip(weights,
modified_durations)])
    return portfolio_modified_duration
# Example usage
weights = [0.4, 0.3, 0.3]
modified_durations = [2.5, 3.8, 4.2]
result = calculate_portfolio_modified_duration(weights,
modified_durations)
print(result)
```

Output
R
[1] 3.4
Python
3.3999999999999995

13. Convexity for a Bond Portfolio

Convexity for a bond portfolio is a measure of the curvature in the relationship between the bond portfolio's price and changes in interest rates. It provides additional insight beyond duration by capturing the non-linear relationship between bond prices and yields. It provides a more accurate estimate of the bond portfolio's price sensitivity.

```
# R
calculate_portfolio_convexity <- function(weights, convexities) {
  portfolio_convexity <- sum(weights * convexities)
  return(portfolio_convexity)
}
# Example usage
weights <- c(0.4, 0.3, 0.3)
convexities <- c(5.2, 6.1, 7.3)
result <- calculate_portfolio_convexity(weights, convexities)
result
```

```
# Python
def calculate_portfolio_convexity(weights, convexities):
    portfolio_convexity = sum([w * c for w, c in zip(weights, convexities)])
    return portfolio_convexity
# Example usage
weights = [0.4, 0.3, 0.3]
convexities = [5.2, 6.1, 7.3]
result = calculate_portfolio_convexity(weights, convexities)
print(result)
```

Output
R
[1] 6.1
Python
6.1

14. Portfolio Yield Based on Bond Yields

Portfolio Yield based on bond yields is a metric that calculates the overall yield of a portfolio by considering the yields of the individual bonds held within that portfolio.

```R
# R
calculate_portfolio_yield <- function(weights, yields) {
  portfolio_yield <- sum(weights * yields)
  return(portfolio_yield)
}
# Example usage
weights <- c(0.4, 0.3, 0.3)
yields <- c(0.04, 0.035, 0.038)
result <- calculate_portfolio_yield(weights, yields)
result
```

```python
# Python
def calculate_portfolio_yield(weights, yields):
    portfolio_yield = sum([w * y for w, y in zip(weights, yields)])
    return portfolio_yield
# Example usage
weights = [0.4, 0.3, 0.3]
yields = [0.04, 0.035, 0.038]
result = calculate_portfolio_yield(weights, yields)
print(result)
```

Output
R
[1] 0.0379
Python
0.0379

15. Bond Equivalent Yield for Semiannual Coupon Bonds

Bond Equivalent Yield (BEY) is a formula used to annualize the yield of a bond with semiannual coupon payments. It is particularly applicable to bonds that pay interest semiannually.

```R
# R
calculate_bey <- function(security_yield) {
  bey_value <- 2 * security_yield
  return(bey_value)
}
# Example usage
security_yield <- 0.05
```

```
result <- calculate_bey(security_yield)
result

# Python
def calculate_bey(security_yield):
    bey_value = 2 * security_yield
    return bey_value
# Example usage
security_yield = 0.05
result = calculate_bey(security_yield)
print(result)
```

Output
R
[1] 0.1
Python
0.1

16. Yield to Worst (YTW) for a Callable Bond

Yield to Worst (YTW) is a measure that calculates the lowest potential yield an investor could receive on a bond, considering various scenarios such as call provisions, prepayments, or sinking fund requirements. For callable bonds, Yield to Worst considers the possibility of the bond being called before maturity.

```
# R
calculate_ytw  <-  function(bond_price, face_value, coupon, periods,
call_price) {
  ytw_value <- ((face_value + (bond_price - call_price)) / 2) ** (1 /
periods) - 1
  return(ytw_value)
}
# Example usage
bond_price <- 950
face_value <- 1000
coupon <- 0.06
periods <- 5
call_price <- 1020
result  <-  calculate_ytw(bond_price, face_value, coupon, periods,
call_price)
result
```

```python
# Python
def calculate_ytw(bond_price, face_value, coupon, periods, call_price):
    ytw_value = ((face_value + (bond_price - call_price)) / 2) ** (1 /
periods) - 1
    return ytw_value
# Example usage
bond_price = 950
face_value = 1000
coupon = 0.06
periods = 5
call_price = 1020
result = calculate_ytw(bond_price, face_value, coupon, periods,
call_price)
print(result)
```

Output
R [1] 2.415785
Python 2.4157854996677854

17. Yield to Worst (YTW) for a Bond Portfolio

Yield to Worst (YTW) for a bond portfolio is the minimum yield an investor can expect from the entire portfolio, considering the worst-case scenarios for each individual bond within the portfolio.

```r
# R
calculate_ytw_portfolio <- function(bond_prices, face_values, coupons,
periods, call_prices) {
  ytw_values <- numeric(length(bond_prices))
  for (i in 1:length(bond_prices)) {
    ytw_values[i] <- ((face_values[i] + (bond_prices[i] - call_prices[i])) /
2) ** (1 / periods[i]) - 1
  }
  return(ytw_values)
}
# Example usage
bond_prices <- c(950, 980, 920)
face_values <- c(1000, 1000, 1000)
coupons <- c(0.06, 0.07, 0.05)
periods <- c(5, 5, 5)
call_prices <- c(1020, 1040, 1000)
```

```r
result <- calculate_ytw_portfolio(bond_prices, face_values, coupons,
periods, call_prices)
result
```

```python
# Python
def calculate_ytw_portfolio(bond_prices, face_values, coupons, periods,
call_prices):
    ytw_values = []
    for i in range(len(bond_prices)):
        ytw_values.append(((face_values[i]      +      (bond_prices[i]      -
call_prices[i])) / 2) ** (1 / periods[i]) - 1)
    return ytw_values
# Example usage
bond_prices = [950, 980, 920]
face_values = [1000, 1000, 1000]
coupons = [0.06, 0.07, 0.05]
periods = [5, 5, 5]
call_prices = [1020, 1040, 1000]
result = calculate_ytw_portfolio(bond_prices, face_values, coupons,
periods, call_prices)
print(result)
```

Output
R
[1] 2.415785 2.423100 2.408408
Python
[2.4157854996677854, 2.4230998825187093, 2.4084079242834604]

18. Spread to Benchmark for a Bond

Spread to Benchmark for a bond refers to the yield spread between the bond's yield and the yield of a benchmark security, typically a government bond with similar maturity. It is a measure of the additional yield that investors demand for taking on the credit risk associated with the specific bond compared to a relatively risk-free benchmark.

```r
# R
calculate_spread_to_benchmark <- function(bond_yield,
benchmark_yield) {
  spread <- bond_yield - benchmark_yield
  return(spread)
}
```

```
# Example usage
bond_yield <- 0.045
benchmark_yield <- 0.035
result <- calculate_spread_to_benchmark(bond_yield, benchmark_yield)
result

# Python
def calculate_spread_to_benchmark(bond_yield, benchmark_yield):
    spread = bond_yield - benchmark_yield
    return spread
# Example usage
bond_yield = 0.045
benchmark_yield = 0.035
result = calculate_spread_to_benchmark(bond_yield, benchmark_yield)
print(result)
```

Output
R [1] 0.01 Python 0.009999999999999995

CHAPTER 8

This chapter consist commonly used code examples for equity valuation calculations in both R and Python:

1. Dividend Discount Model (DDM) Valuation

DDM is that the present value of all future dividends represents the fair value of the stock. It provides a simple framework for estimating the fair value of a stock based on expected future dividends and their growth rate.

```r
# R
calculate_ddm_valuation <- function(dividend, discount_rate, growth_rate) {
  valuation <- dividend / (discount_rate - growth_rate)
  return(valuation)
}
# Example usage
dividend <- 2.5
discount_rate <- 0.1
growth_rate <- 0.05
result <- calculate_ddm_valuation(dividend, discount_rate, growth_rate)
result
```

```python
# Python
def calculate_ddm_valuation(dividend, discount_rate, growth_rate):
    valuation = dividend / (discount_rate - growth_rate)
    return valuation
# Example usage
dividend = 2.5
discount_rate = 0.1
growth_rate = 0.05
result = calculate_ddm_valuation(dividend, discount_rate, growth_rate)
print(result)
```

Output
R
[1] 50
Python
50.0

2. Price-to-Earnings (P/E) Ratio

The Price-to-Earnings (P/E) ratio is a financial metric used to assess the valuation of a company's stock by comparing its current market price per share to its earnings per share (EPS).

```r
# R
calculate_pe_ratio <- function(stock_price, earnings_per_share) {
  pe_ratio <- stock_price / earnings_per_share
  return(pe_ratio)
}
# Example usage
stock_price <- 50
earnings_per_share <- 5
result <- calculate_pe_ratio(stock_price, earnings_per_share)
result
```

```python
# Python
def calculate_pe_ratio(stock_price, earnings_per_share):
    pe_ratio = stock_price / earnings_per_share
    return pe_ratio
# Example usage
stock_price = 50
earnings_per_share = 5
result = calculate_pe_ratio(stock_price, earnings_per_share)
print(result)
```

Output
R
[1] 10
Python
10.0

3. Price-to-Book (P/B) Ratio

The Price-to-Book (P/B) ratio is a financial metric used to assess the valuation of a company by comparing its market price per share to its book value per share. The P/B ratio is a key indicator of how the market values a company's assets relative to its market capitalization.

```r
# R
calculate_pb_ratio <- function(stock_price, book_value_per_share) {
  pb_ratio <- stock_price / book_value_per_share
  return(pb_ratio)
}
# Example usage
stock_price <- 60
book_value_per_share <- 10
result <- calculate_pb_ratio(stock_price, book_value_per_share)
result
```

```python
# Python
def calculate_pb_ratio(stock_price, book_value_per_share):
    pb_ratio = stock_price / book_value_per_share
    return pb_ratio
# Example usage
stock_price = 60
book_value_per_share = 10
result = calculate_pb_ratio(stock_price, book_value_per_share)
print(result)
```

Output
R
[1] 6
Python
6.0

4. Price-to-Sales (P/S) Ratio

The Price-to-Sales (P/S) ratio is a financial metric used to assess the valuation of a company by comparing its market capitalization to its total revenue or sales. The P/S ratio is a key indicator of how the market values a company's sales relative to its market value.

```r
# R
calculate_ps_ratio <- function(stock_price, revenue_per_share) {
  ps_ratio <- stock_price / revenue_per_share
  return(ps_ratio)
}
# Example usage
stock_price <- 50
```

```r
revenue_per_share <- 20
result <- calculate_ps_ratio(stock_price, revenue_per_share)
result
```

```python
# Python
def calculate_ps_ratio(stock_price, revenue_per_share):
    ps_ratio = stock_price / revenue_per_share
    return ps_ratio
# Example usage
stock_price = 50
revenue_per_share = 20
result = calculate_ps_ratio(stock_price, revenue_per_share)
print(result)
```

Output
R
[1] 2.5
Python
2.5

5. Enterprise Value (EV)

Enterprise Value (EV) represents the total value of a company, considering not only its market capitalization but also its debt, cash, and other non-equity sources of financing.

```r
# R
calculate_enterprise_value <- function(market_cap, total_debt,
cash_and_equivalents) {
  enterprise_value <- market_cap + total_debt - cash_and_equivalents
  return(enterprise_value)
}
# Example usage
market_cap <- 5000000000
total_debt <- 2000000000
cash_and_equivalents <- 1000000000
result <- calculate_enterprise_value(market_cap, total_debt,
cash_and_equivalents)
result
```

```python
# Python
def calculate_enterprise_value(market_cap, total_debt,
cash_and_equivalents):
    enterprise_value = market_cap + total_debt - cash_and_equivalents
    return enterprise_value
# Example usage
market_cap = 5000000000
total_debt = 2000000000
cash_and_equivalents = 1000000000
result = calculate_enterprise_value(market_cap, total_debt,
cash_and_equivalents)
print(result)
```

Output
R
[1] 6e+09
Python
6000000000

6. Earnings Before Interest and Taxes (EBIT)

Earnings Before Interest and Taxes (EBIT) represents a company's operating profit, calculated by subtracting its operating expenses (excluding interest and taxes) from its revenue. EBIT is a measure of a company's profitability before considering the impact of interest and taxes.

```r
# R
calculate_ebit <- function(revenue, operating_expenses) {
  ebit <- revenue - operating_expenses
  return(ebit)
}
# Example usage
revenue <- 10000000
operating_expenses <- 6000000
result <- calculate_ebit(revenue, operating_expenses)
result
```

```python
# Python
def calculate_ebit(revenue, operating_expenses):
    ebit = revenue - operating_expenses
    return ebit
```

```
# Example usage
revenue = 10000000
operating_expenses = 6000000
result = calculate_ebit(revenue, operating_expenses)
print(result)
```

Output
R
[1] 4e+06
Python
4000000

7. EBITDA

Earnings Before Interest, Taxes, Depreciation, and Amortization (EBITDA) metric represents a company's operating performance and profitability by excluding certain non-cash and non-operating expenses. It provides a measure of a company's ability to generate cash from its core business operations.

```
# R
calculate_ebitda <- function(revenue, operating_expenses, depreciation,
amortization) {
  ebitda <- revenue - operating_expenses + depreciation + amortization
  return(ebitda)
}
# Example usage
revenue <- 10000000
operating_expenses <- 6000000
depreciation <- 2000000
amortization <- 1000000
result <- calculate_ebitda(revenue, operating_expenses, depreciation,
amortization)
result
```

```
# Python
def calculate_ebitda(revenue, operating_expenses, depreciation,
amortization):
  ebitda = revenue - operating_expenses + depreciation + amortization
  return ebitda
# Example usage
```

```
revenue = 10000000
operating_expenses = 6000000
depreciation = 2000000
amortization = 1000000
result = calculate_ebitda(revenue, operating_expenses, depreciation,
amortization)
print(result)
```

Output
R
[1] 7e+06
Python
7000000

8. Free Cash Flow (FCF)

FCF represents the cash generated by a company's operations that is available for distribution to investors, creditors, and reinvestment in the business. It is a measure of a company's ability to generate cash after accounting for capital expenditures necessary to maintain or expand its asset base.

```
# R
calculate_fcf <- function(net_income, depreciation,
changes_in_working_capital, capital_expenditure) {
  fcf <- net_income + depreciation - changes_in_working_capital -
capital_expenditure
  return(fcf)
}
# Example usage
net_income <- 5000000
depreciation <- 1000000
changes_in_working_capital <- 2000000
capital_expenditure <- 1500000
result <- calculate_fcf(net_income, depreciation,
changes_in_working_capital, capital_expenditure)
result
```

```
# Python
def calculate_fcf(net_income, depreciation, changes_in_working_capital,
capital_expenditure):
```

```
  fcf = net_income + depreciation - changes_in_working_capital -
capital_expenditure
  return fcf
# Example usage
net_income = 5000000
depreciation = 1000000
changes_in_working_capital = 2000000
capital_expenditure = 1500000
result      =      calculate_fcf(net_income,      depreciation,
changes_in_working_capital, capital_expenditure)
print(result)
```

Output
R
[1] 2500000
Python
2500000

9. Return on Equity (ROE)

Return on Equity measures the profitability of a company by evaluating
how efficiently it utilizes its shareholders' equity to generate profits. ROE
is expressed as a percentage and is calculated by dividing a company's net
income by its average shareholders' equity.

```
# R
calculate_roe <- function(net_income, average_equity) {
  roe <- net_income / average_equity
  return(roe)
}
# Example usage
net_income <- 5000000
average_equity <- 3000000
result <- calculate_roe(net_income, average_equity)
result
```

```
# Python
def calculate_roe(net_income, average_equity):
  roe = net_income / average_equity
  return roe
# Example usage
net_income = 5000000
```

```
average_equity = 3000000
result = calculate_roe(net_income, average_equity)
print(result)
```

Output
R
[1] 1.666667
Python
1.6666666666666667

10. Return on Assets (ROA)

Return on Assets measures a company's efficiency in generating profits from its assets. It evaluates how well a company utilizes its assets to generate earnings. ROA is expressed as a percentage and is calculated by dividing a company's net income by its average total assets.

```
# R
calculate_roa <- function(net_income, average_total_assets) {
  roa <- net_income / average_total_assets
  return(roa)
}
# Example usage
net_income <- 5000000
average_total_assets <- 20000000
result <- calculate_roa(net_income, average_total_assets)
result
```

```
# Python
def calculate_roa(net_income, average_total_assets):
    roa = net_income / average_total_assets
    return roa
# Example usage
net_income = 5000000
average_total_assets = 20000000
result = calculate_roa(net_income, average_total_assets)
print(result)
```

Output
R [1] 0.25
Python 0.25

11. Dividend Yield

Dividend Yield indicates the annual dividend income expressed as a percentage of a company's stock price. It provides investors with insights into the return they can expect from dividend payments relative to the current market value of the stock.

```
# R
calculate_dividend_yield <- function(dividends, stock_price) {
  dividend_yield <- dividends / stock_price
  return(dividend_yield)
}
# Example usage
dividends <- 1
stock_price <- 50
result <- calculate_dividend_yield(dividends, stock_price)
result
```

```
# Python
def calculate_dividend_yield(dividends, stock_price):
    dividend_yield = dividends / stock_price
    return dividend_yield
# Example usage
dividends = 1
stock_price = 50
result = calculate_dividend_yield(dividends, stock_price)
print(result)
```

Output
R
[1] 0.02
Python
0.02

12. Capital Asset Pricing Model (CAPM) Expected Return

CAPM provides an estimate of the expected return on an investment, typically a stock, based on its systematic risk or beta. The expected return according to CAPM is calculated using the following formula:

Expected Return=Risk-Free Rate+β×(Market Return−Risk-Free Rate)

```R
# R
calculate_capm_expected_return <- function(risk_free_rate, market_return, beta) {
 capm_expected_return <- risk_free_rate + beta * (market_return - risk_free_rate)
 return(capm_expected_return)
}
# Example usage
risk_free_rate <- 0.02
market_return <- 0.08
beta <- 1.2
result <- calculate_capm_expected_return(risk_free_rate, market_return, beta)
result
```

```python
# Python
def calculate_capm_expected_return(risk_free_rate, market_return, beta):
   capm_expected_return = risk_free_rate + beta * (market_return - risk_free_rate)
   return capm_expected_return
# Example usage
risk_free_rate = 0.02
market_return = 0.08
beta = 1.2
result = calculate_capm_expected_return(risk_free_rate, market_return, beta)
print(result)
```

Output
R [1] 0.092
Python 0.092

13. Weighted Average Cost of Capital (WACC)

WACC represents the average cost of capital for a company, considering the proportion of each type of capital used. It is a weighted average of the cost of equity, debt, and any other sources of capital.

```r
# R
calculate_wacc <- function(equity_value, debt_value, equity_cost, debt_cost, tax_rate) {
  total_value <- equity_value + debt_value
  equity_weight <- equity_value / total_value
  debt_weight <- debt_value / total_value
  wacc <- (equity_weight * equity_cost) + (debt_weight * debt_cost * (1 - tax_rate))
  return(wacc)
}
# Example usage
equity_value <- 5000000
debt_value <- 3000000
equity_cost <- 0.12
debt_cost <- 0.05
tax_rate <- 0.3
```

```python
# Python
def calculate_wacc(equity_value, debt_value, equity_cost, debt_cost, tax_rate):
    total_value = equity_value + debt_value
    equity_weight = equity_value / total_value
    debt_weight = debt_value / total_value
    wacc = (equity_weight * equity_cost) + (debt_weight * debt_cost * (1 - tax_rate))
    return wacc
# Example usage
equity_value = 5000000
debt_value = 3000000
equity_cost = 0.12
debt_cost = 0.05
tax_rate = 0.3
result = calculate_wacc(equity_value, debt_value, equity_cost, debt_cost, tax_rate)
print(result)
```

Output
R
[1] 0.088125
Python
0.088125

14. Intrinsic Value using the Two-Stage DDM

Two stage DDM is a method for estimating the fair value of a stock based on its expected future dividend payments. The Two-Stage DDM considers two distinct phases of a company's dividend growth: an initial "high-growth" phase followed by a "stable", lower-growth phase.

```r
# R
calculate_intrinsic_value <- function(dividends, growth_rate1,
growth_rate2, discount_rate) {
  # Calculate present value of dividends during the high growth phase
  present_value_high_growth <- sum(dividends * (1 +
growth_rate1)^(0:(length(dividends)-1)) / (1 +
discount_rate)^(0:(length(dividends)-1)))
  # Calculate present value of dividends during the stable growth phase
  stable_growth_dividend <- dividends[length(dividends)] * (1 +
growth_rate1)
  present_value_stable_growth <- stable_growth_dividend /
(discount_rate - growth_rate2)
  intrinsic_value <- present_value_high_growth +
present_value_stable_growth
  return(intrinsic_value)
}
# Example usage in R
dividends <- c(2, 2.5, 3, 3.5, 4)
growth_rate1 <- 0.1 #which is high growth rate
growth_rate2 <- 0.05 #stable growth rate
discount_rate <- 0.08
result_r <- calculate_intrinsic_value(dividends, growth_rate1,
growth_rate2, discount_rate)
print(result_r)

# Python
def calculate_intrinsic_value(dividends, growth_rate1, growth_rate2,
discount_rate):
```

212

```python
# Calculate present value of dividends during the high growth phase
present_value_high_growth = sum([dividends[i] * (1 +
growth_rate1)**i / (1 + discount_rate)**i for i in range(len(dividends))])
# Calculate present value of dividends during the stable growth phase
stable_growth_dividend = dividends[-1] * (1 + growth_rate1)
present_value_stable_growth = stable_growth_dividend /
(discount_rate - growth_rate2)
intrinsic_value = present_value_high_growth +
present_value_stable_growth
return intrinsic_value
# Example usage in Python
dividends = [2, 2.5, 3, 3.5, 4]
growth_rate1 = 0.1 #which is high growth rate
growth_rate2 = 0.05 #stable growth rate
discount_rate = 0.08
result_python = calculate_intrinsic_value(dividends, growth_rate1,
growth_rate2, discount_rate)
print(result_python)
```

Output
R
[1] 162.3278
Python
162.32779920536808

CHAPTER 9

This chapter covers commonly used code examples for alternative investment calculations in both R and Python. Alternative investments refer to a diverse set of investment options beyond traditional stocks, bonds, and cash. These investments often deviate from conventional asset classes and may include a wide range of opportunities. Private equity, hedge funds, real estate, commodities, venture capital, private debt, collectibles, cryptocurrencies and blockchain, infrastructure investments, and structured products are some common types of alternative investments.

1. Net Present Value of an Alternative Investment

The Net Present Value (NPV) of an alternative investment is a financial metric used to evaluate the profitability of an investment opportunity. NPV represents the difference between the present value of cash inflows and the present value of cash outflows over a specific time, typically the lifespan of the investment.

```
#R
calculate_npv <- function(cash_flows, discount_rate) {
  npv_value <- sum(cash_flows / (1 +
discount_rate)^(0:(length(cash_flows)-1)))
  return(npv_value)
}
# Example usage in R
cash_flows <- c(-1000, 200, 300, 400, 500)
discount_rate <- 0.1
result_r <- calculate_npv(cash_flows, discount_rate)
print(result_r)
```

And the corresponding Python code:

```
# Python
def calculate_npv(cash_flows, discount_rate):
    npv_value = sum([cf / (1 + discount_rate)**i for i, cf in
enumerate(cash_flows)])
    return npv_value
# Example usage in Python
cash_flows = [-1000, 200, 300, 400, 500]
```

```
discount_rate = 0.1
result_python = calculate_npv(cash_flows, discount_rate)
print(result_python)
```
Output
R
[1] 71.78471
Python
71.78471415886867

2. Internal Rate of Return of an Alternative Investment

IRR of an alternative investment is a financial metric that represents the discount rate at which the net present value of the investment becomes zero. It is the rate of return at which the present value of expected future cash inflows equals the present value of the initial investment.

```
# R
cash_flows <- c(-1000, 200, 300, 400, 500)
irr_value <- uniroot(function(rate) sum(cash_flows / (1 +
rate)^(0:(length(cash_flows) - 1))), interval = c(0, 1))$root
print(irr_value)
```

```
# Python
import numpy_financial as npf
# Example cash flows
cash_flows = [-100, 30, 35, 40, 50]
# Calculate IRR using numpy_financial
irr_value = npf.irr(cash_flows)
# Print the result
print(f"Internal Rate of Return (IRR): {irr_value:.4%}")
```

Output
R
[1] 0.1282636
Python
Internal Rate of Return (IRR): 18.3273%

3. Payback Period of an Alternative Investment

The Payback Period of an alternative investment represents the amount of time it takes for the initial investment in a project to be recovered through the project's expected cash inflows. It is the time it takes for an investment to "pay back" its initial cost.

```R
#R
# Function to calculate Payback Period
payback_period <- function(cash_flows) {
  cumulative_cash_flows <- cumsum(cash_flows)
# Find the index where cumulative cash flow becomes positive or zero
  payback_index <- which(cumulative_cash_flows >= 0)[1]
# Calculate payback period
  payback_period_value <- payback_index - 1 +
(cumulative_cash_flows[payback_index - 1] /
cash_flows[payback_index])
  return(payback_period_value)
}
# Example cash flows
cash_flows <- c(-100, 20, 30, 40, 50)
# Calculate Payback Period
payback_period_value <- payback_period(cash_flows)
print(paste("Payback Period:", round(payback_period_value, 2)))
```

```Python
#Python
# Function to calculate Payback Period
def payback_period(cash_flows):
    cumulative_cash_flows = [sum(cash_flows[:i + 1]) for i in
range(len(cash_flows))]
# Find the index where cumulative cash flow becomes positive or zero
payback_index = next(i for i, value in
enumerate(cumulative_cash_flows) if value >= 0)
# Calculate payback period
    payback_period_value = payback_index - 1 +
(abs(cumulative_cash_flows[payback_index - 1]) /
cash_flows[payback_index])
    return payback_period_value
# Example cash flows
cash_flows = [-100, 20, 30, 40, 50, 10]
# Calculate Payback Period
```

216

```
payback_period_value = payback_period(cash_flows)
print(f"Payback Period: {round(payback_period_value, 2)} years")
```

Output
R
[1] "Payback Period: 3.8"
Python
Payback Period: 3.8 years

4. Return on Investment (ROI) of an Alternative Investment

ROI of an alternative investment measures the profitability of an investment relative to its initial cost. It is expressed as a percentage and represents the gain or loss generated on an investment in relation to the amount invested.

```
#R
# Function to calculate Return on Investment (ROI)
calculate_roi <- function(initial_investment, final_value) {
  roi <- ((final_value - initial_investment) / initial_investment) * 100
  return(roi)
}
# Example values
initial_investment <- 1000
final_value <- 1500
# Calculate ROI
roi_value <- calculate_roi(initial_investment, final_value)
print(paste("Return on Investment (ROI):", round(roi_value, 2), "%"))
```

```
#Python
# Function to calculate Return on Investment (ROI)
def calculate_roi(initial_investment, final_value):
    roi = ((final_value - initial_investment) / initial_investment) * 100
    return roi
# Example values
initial_investment = 1000
final_value = 1500
# Calculate ROI
roi_value = calculate_roi(initial_investment, final_value)
print(f"Return on Investment (ROI): {round(roi_value, 2)}%")
```

Output
R
[1] "Return on Investment (ROI): 50 %"
Python
Return on Investment (ROI): 50.0%

5. Modified Duration of an Alternative Investment

Modified Duration measures the sensitivity of the price of fixed-income investment to changes in interest rates. It is a modified or adjusted version of Macaulay Duration that considers the approximate percentage change in the bond's price for a 1% change in yield.

```r
# R
calculate_modified_duration <- function(cash_flows, discount_rate,
yield_change) {
 n <- length(cash_flows)
 modified_duration <- sum((1:n) * cash_flows / (1 +
discount_rate)^((1:n) + yield_change))
 return(modified_duration)
}
# Example in R
cash_flows <- c(-1000, 100, 100, 100, 100, 1100)
discount_rate <- 0.05
yield_change <- 0.01
modified_duration_r <- calculate_modified_duration(cash_flows,
discount_rate, yield_change)
print(modified_duration_r)
```

```python
# Python
import numpy as np
def calculate_modified_duration(cash_flows, discount_rate,
yield_change):
    n = len(cash_flows)
    modified_duration = np.sum((np.arange(1, n + 1) * cash_flows) / (1 +
discount_rate)**(np.arange(1, n + 1) + yield_change))
    return modified_duration
# Example in Python
cash_flows = [-1000, 100, 100, 100, 100, 1100]
discount_rate = 0.05
yield_change = 0.01
```

```
modified_duration_python = calculate_modified_duration(cash_flows,
discount_rate, yield_change)
print(modified_duration_python)
```

Output
R
[1] 5131.538
Python
5131.537617319409

6. Real Estate Capitalization Rate (Cap Rate)

The Real Estate Capitalization Rate is used in real estate to evaluate the
potential profitability and risk of an investment property. It is calculated
by dividing the property's net operating income by its current market value
or acquisition cost and is expressed as a percentage.

```
# R
calculate_cap_rate <- function(net_operating_income, property_value) {
  cap_rate <- (net_operating_income / property_value) * 100
  return(cap_rate)
}
# Example in R
net_operating_income <- 120000
property_value <- 1500000
cap_rate_r <- calculate_cap_rate(net_operating_income, property_value)
print(cap_rate_r)
```

```
# Python
def calculate_cap_rate(net_operating_income, property_value):
    cap_rate = (net_operating_income / property_value) * 100
    return cap_rate
# Example in Python
net_operating_income = 120000
property_value = 1500000
cap_rate_python = calculate_cap_rate(net_operating_income,
property_value)
print(cap_rate_python)
```

Output
R [1] 8
Python 8.0

7. Real Estate Cash-on-Cash Return

Real Estate Cash-on-Cash Return is used in real estate investment to evaluate the annual pre-tax cash flow relative to the total amount of cash invested in a property. It provides investors with a percentage that represents the return generated on the actual cash invested in the property.

```r
# R
calculate_cash_on_cash_return <- function(net_cash_flow,
total_cash_investment) {
  cash_on_cash_return <- (net_cash_flow / total_cash_investment) * 100
  return(cash_on_cash_return)
}
# Example in R
net_cash_flow <- 50000
total_cash_investment <- 400000
cash_on_cash_return_r <-
calculate_cash_on_cash_return(net_cash_flow, total_cash_investment)
print(cash_on_cash_return_r)
```

```python
# Python
def calculate_cash_on_cash_return(net_cash_flow,
total_cash_investment):
    cash_on_cash_return = (net_cash_flow / total_cash_investment) * 100
    return cash_on_cash_return
# Example in Python
net_cash_flow = 50000
total_cash_investment = 400000
cash_on_cash_return_python =
calculate_cash_on_cash_return(net_cash_flow, total_cash_investment)
print(cash_on_cash_return_python)
```

Output
R
[1] 12.5
Python
12.5

8. Rental Yield for Real Estate Investment

Rental Yield is used in real estate investment to assess the potential return generated from rental income relative to the property's value. It provides investors with a percentage that represents the income generated through renting out the property.

```r
# R
calculate_rental_yield <- function(annual_rental_income,
property_value) {
  rental_yield <- (annual_rental_income / property_value) * 100
  return(rental_yield)
}
# Example in R
annual_rental_income <- 25000
property_value <- 500000
rental_yield_r <- calculate_rental_yield(annual_rental_income,
property_value)
print(rental_yield_r)
```

```python
# Python
def calculate_rental_yield(annual_rental_income, property_value):
    rental_yield = (annual_rental_income / property_value) * 100
    return rental_yield
# Example in Python
annual_rental_income = 25000
property_value = 500000
rental_yield_python = calculate_rental_yield(annual_rental_income,
property_value)
print(rental_yield_python)
```

Output
R
[1] 5
Python
5.0

9. Private Equity Multiple (DPI, RVPI, TVPI)

Private Equity Multiple, often referred to as TVPI (Total Value to Paid-In), is a performance metric used in private equity investments to assess the overall value generated relative to the amount of capital invested. The Private Equity Multiple is comprised of three components: DPI (Distributions to Paid-In), RVPI (Residual Value to Paid-In), and TVPI (Total Value to Paid-In).

```R
# R
calculate_private_equity_multiple <- function(distributed, contributed, residual_value) {
  dpi <- distributed / contributed
  rvpi <- residual_value / contributed
  tvpi <- (distributed + residual_value) / contributed
  return(c(dpi = dpi, rvpi = rvpi, tvpi = tvpi))
}
# Example in R
distributed <- 1500000
contributed <- 1000000
residual_value <- 500000
private_equity_multiple_r <-
calculate_private_equity_multiple(distributed, contributed, residual_value)
print(private_equity_multiple_r)
```

```Python
# Python
def calculate_private_equity_multiple(distributed, contributed, residual_value):
    dpi = distributed / contributed
    rvpi = residual_value / contributed
    tvpi = (distributed + residual_value) / contributed
    return {"dpi": dpi, "rvpi": rvpi, "tvpi": tvpi}
# Example in Python
distributed = 1500000
contributed = 1000000
residual_value = 500000
private_equity_multiple_python =
calculate_private_equity_multiple(distributed, contributed, residual_value)
print(private_equity_multiple_python)
```

Output
R
dpi rvpi tvpi
1.5 0.5 2.0
Python
{'dpi': 1.5, 'rvpi': 0.5, 'tvpi': 2.0}

11. Hedge Fund Sharpe Ratio

The Hedge Fund Sharpe Ratio is a risk-adjusted performance measure used to evaluate the return of a hedge fund relative to its level of risk. It helps investors assess the efficiency of an investment strategy by considering both the return achieved and the level of risk taken.

```r
# R
calculate_sharpe_ratio <- function(returns, risk_free_rate) {
  excess_returns <- returns - risk_free_rate
  sharpe_ratio <- mean(excess_returns) / sd(excess_returns) * sqrt(252)
# Assuming 252 trading days in a year
  return(sharpe_ratio)
}
# Example in R
hedge_fund_returns <- c(0.02, 0.03, -0.01, 0.015, 0.025)
risk_free_rate <- 0.01
sharpe_ratio_r <- calculate_sharpe_ratio(hedge_fund_returns,
risk_free_rate)
print(sharpe_ratio_r)
```

```python
# Python
import numpy as np
def calculate_sharpe_ratio(returns, risk_free_rate):
    excess_returns = returns - risk_free_rate
    sharpe_ratio = np.mean(excess_returns) / np.std(excess_returns) *
np.sqrt(252)  # Assuming 252 trading days in a year
    return sharpe_ratio
# Example in Python
hedge_fund_returns = np.array([0.02, 0.03, -0.01, 0.015, 0.025])
risk_free_rate = 0.01
sharpe_ratio_python = calculate_sharpe_ratio(hedge_fund_returns,
risk_free_rate)
print(sharpe_ratio_python)
```

Output
R
[1] 6.116397
Python
6.838339462028639

12. Hedge Fund Sortino Ratio

The Hedge Fund Sortino Ratio is a variation of the traditional "Sharpe Ratio", designed to provide a more focused evaluation of a hedge fund's risk-adjusted performance by considering only the downside risk. Sortino Ratio is particularly useful in assessing how well a hedge fund is delivering returns relative to the downside volatility.

```r
# R
calculate_sortino_ratio <- function(returns, risk_free_rate, target_return)
{
  downside_returns <- pmin(returns - target_return, 0)
  downside_deviation <- sqrt(mean(downside_returns^2))
  sortino_ratio <- (mean(returns) - risk_free_rate) / downside_deviation
  return(sortino_ratio)
}
# Example in R
hedge_fund_returns <- c(0.02, 0.03, -0.01, 0.015, 0.025)
risk_free_rate <- 0.01
target_return <- 0.001
sortino_ratio_r      <-      calculate_sortino_ratio(hedge_fund_returns,
risk_free_rate, target_return)
print(sortino_ratio_r)
```

```python
# Python
import numpy as np
def calculate_sortino_ratio(returns, risk_free_rate, target_return):
    downside_returns = np.minimum(returns - target_return, 0)
    downside_deviation = np.sqrt(np.mean(downside_returns**2))
    sortino_ratio    =    (np.mean(returns)    -    risk_free_rate)    /
downside_deviation
    return sortino_ratio
# Example in Python
hedge_fund_returns = np.array([0.02, 0.03, -0.01, 0.015, 0.025])
risk_free_rate = 0.01
```

```
target_return = 0.001
sortino_ratio_python    =    calculate_sortino_ratio(hedge_fund_returns,
risk_free_rate, target_return)
print(sortino_ratio_python)
```

Output
R
[1] 1.219673
Python
1.2196734422726125

13. Cryptocurrency Volatility

Cryptocurrency volatility refers to the degree of variation or fluctuation in the price of a cryptocurrency over a specific period. It is a measure of how much the price of a cryptocurrency deviates from its average value.

Examples for ETH-USD data from = "2022-01-01", to "2023-01-01 which use yahoo finance data

```
# R
if (!requireNamespace("quantmod", quietly = TRUE)) {
  install.packages("quantmod")
}
library(quantmod)
# Function to calculate cryptocurrency volatility
calculate_crypto_volatility <- function(ticker_symbol) {
  # Download historical data using quantmod
  getSymbols(ticker_symbol, src = "yahoo", from = "2022-01-01", to =
"2023-01-01", auto.assign = TRUE)
  # Extract adjusted close prices
  crypto_prices <- Cl(get(ticker_symbol))
  # Calculate daily returns
  crypto_returns <- diff(log(crypto_prices))
  # Remove NA values
  crypto_returns <- crypto_returns[!is.na(crypto_returns)]
  # Calculate volatility (annualized)
  crypto_volatility <- sd(crypto_returns) * sqrt(252)  # Assuming 252
trading days in a year
  return(crypto_volatility)
}
```

```r
# Example for Ethereum (ETH)
eth_volatility <- calculate_crypto_volatility("ETH-USD")
print(paste("Ethereum Volatility:", eth_volatility))
```

```python
#Python
pip install yfinance
import yfinance as yf
import numpy as np
def calculate_crypto_volatility(ticker_symbol):
    # Fetch historical data from Yahoo Finance for the last year
    crypto_data = yf.download(ticker_symbol, start="2022-01-01", end="2023-01-01")
    # Calculate daily returns
    crypto_returns = crypto_data['Adj Close'].pct_change().dropna()
    # Calculate volatility (annualized)
    crypto_volatility = np.std(crypto_returns) * np.sqrt(252)  # Assuming 252 trading days in a year
    return crypto_volatility
# Example for Ethereum (ETH)
eth_volatility = calculate_crypto_volatility("ETH-USD")
print(f"Ethereum Volatility: {eth_volatility:.4f}")
```

Output
R
[1] "Ethereum Volatility: 0.72370094424837"
Python
Ethereum Volatility: 0.7175

14. Venture Capital Return Multiple (TVPI)

The Venture Capital Return Multiple is a measure used in the field of venture capital to assess the overall performance and returns generated by a venture capital fund.

```r
#R
# Function to calculate Venture Capital Return Multiple
calculate_vc_return_multiple <- function(total_distributions, total_invested_capital) {
  vc_return_multiple <- total_distributions / total_invested_capital
  return(vc_return_multiple)
}
# Example values
```

```
total_distributions <- 5000000  # Replace with actual total distributions
total_invested_capital <- 2000000  # Replace with actual total invested
capital
# Calculate Venture Capital Return Multiple in R
vc_return_multiple <- calculate_vc_return_multiple(total_distributions,
total_invested_capital)
print(paste("Venture Capital Return Multiple (R):", vc_return_multiple))
```

```
#Python
# Function to calculate Venture Capital Return Multiple
def                 calculate_vc_return_multiple(total_distributions,
total_invested_capital):
    vc_return_multiple = total_distributions / total_invested_capital
    return vc_return_multiple
# Example values
total_distributions = 5000000  # Replace with actual total distributions
total_invested_capital = 2000000  # Replace with actual total invested
capital
# Calculate Venture Capital Return Multiple in Python
vc_return_multiple  =  calculate_vc_return_multiple(total_distributions,
total_invested_capital)
print("Venture Capital Return Multiple (Python):", vc_return_multiple)
```

Output
R
[1] "Venture Capital Return Multiple (R): 2.5"
Python
Venture Capital Return Multiple (Python): 2.5

15. Infrastructure Investment Yield

Infrastructure investment yield refers to the return or income generated by
investing in infrastructure assets. Infrastructure investment yield may be
derived from dividends or distributions, toll and usage fees, lease
payments, government contracts or payments, and potential capital
appreciation over time.

```
#R
# Function to calculate Infrastructure Investment Yield
calculate_infrastructure_yield <- function(annual_income,
total_invested_capital) {
```

```r
  infrastructure_yield <- annual_income / total_invested_capital
  return(infrastructure_yield)
}
# Example values
annual_income <- 1000000  # Replace with actual annual income
total_invested_capital <- 15000000  # Replace with actual total invested
capital
# Calculate Infrastructure Investment Yield in R
infrastructure_yield <- calculate_infrastructure_yield(annual_income,
total_invested_capital)
print(paste("Infrastructure Investment Yield (R):", infrastructure_yield))
```

```python
#Python
# Function to calculate Infrastructure Investment Yield
def calculate_infrastructure_yield(annual_income,
total_invested_capital):
    infrastructure_yield = annual_income / total_invested_capital
    return infrastructure_yield
# Example values
annual_income = 1000000  # Replace with actual annual income
total_invested_capital = 15000000  # Replace with actual total invested
capital
# Calculate Infrastructure Investment Yield in Python
infrastructure_yield = calculate_infrastructure_yield(annual_income,
total_invested_capital)
print("Infrastructure Investment Yield (Python):", infrastructure_yield)
```

Output
R
[1] "Infrastructure Investment Yield (R): 0.0666666666666667"
Python
Infrastructure Investment Yield (Python): 0.06666666666666667

16. Art Investment Return

Art investment return refers to the financial gains or losses realized from investing in works of art. Art investment return is driven by capital appreciation based on factors like artist reputation and market demand, realized through sales or auctions; potential income from renting or leasing artworks; diversification benefits in a portfolio; and the personal enjoyment derived from owning and appreciating the art pieces.

```r
#R Example
# Function to calculate Art Investment Return
calculate_art_investment_return <- function(initial_value, final_value,
investment_period_years) {
  annualized_return = ((final_value /
initial_value)^(1/investment_period_years)) - 1
  return(annualized_return)
}
# Example values
initial_value <- 50000  # Replace with the initial value of the art
investment
final_value <- 200000  # Replace with the final value of the art
investment after the investment period
investment_period_years <- 30  # Replace with the investment period in
years
# Calculate Art Investment Return in R
art_return <- calculate_art_investment_return(initial_value, final_value,
investment_period_years)
print(paste("Annualized Art Investment Return (R):", art_return))
```

```python
#Python Example
# Function to calculate Art Investment Return
def calculate_art_investment_return(initial_value, final_value,
investment_period_years):
    annualized_return = ((final_value / initial_value) ** (1 /
investment_period_years)) - 1
    return annualized_return
# Example values
initial_value = 50000  # Replace with the initial value of the art
investment
final_value = 200000  # Replace with the final value of the art
investment after the investment period
investment_period_years = 30  # Replace with the investment period in
years
# Calculate Art Investment Return in Python
art_return = calculate_art_investment_return(initial_value, final_value,
investment_period_years)
print("Annualized Art Investment Return (Python):", art_return)
```

Output
R
[1] "Annualized Art Investment Return (R): 0.0472941228206267"
Python
Annualized Art Investment Return (Python): 0.04729412282062673

17. Peer-to-Peer Lending ROI

Peer-to-peer (P2P) lending Return on Investment refers to the financial gain or loss an investor experiences from participating in a P2P lending platform. This is typically calculated by considering the interest earned from loans minus any associated fees and defaults, divided by the initial investment, and expressed as a percentage.

```r
#R Example
# Function to calculate P2P Lending ROI
calculate_p2p_lending_roi <- function(initial_investment,
interest_earned, fees_paid) {
  total_return = interest_earned - fees_paid
  roi = (total_return / initial_investment) * 100
  return(roi)
}
# Example values
initial_investment <- 10000  # Replace with the initial investment in P2P
lending
interest_earned <- 2500  # Replace with the total interest earned
fees_paid <- 200  # Replace with any fees paid during the investment
period
# Calculate P2P Lending ROI in R
p2p_roi <- calculate_p2p_lending_roi(initial_investment,
interest_earned, fees_paid)
print(paste("P2P Lending ROI (R):", p2p_roi, "%"))
```

```python
#Python Example
# Function to calculate P2P Lending ROI
def calculate_p2p_lending_roi(initial_investment, interest_earned,
fees_paid):
    total_return = interest_earned - fees_paid
    roi = (total_return / initial_investment) * 100
    return roi
# Example values
```

```
initial_investment = 10000  # Replace with the initial investment in P2P
lending
interest_earned = 2500  # Replace with the total interest earned
fees_paid = 200  # Replace with any fees paid during the investment
period
# Calculate P2P Lending ROI in Python
p2p_roi = calculate_p2p_lending_roi(initial_investment, interest_earned,
fees_paid)
print("P2P Lending ROI (Python):", p2p_roi, "%")
```

Output
R
[1] "P2P Lending ROI (R): 23 %"
Python
P2P Lending ROI (Python): 23.0 %

18. Precious Metals Investment Return

Precious metals investment return refers to the financial gain or loss that
an investor experiences from investing in precious metals such as gold,
silver, platinum, or palladium. The return is typically calculated based on
the change in the value of the precious metal investment over a specific
period with related fees or transaction costs.

```
#R Example
# Function to calculate Precious Metals Investment Return
calculate_metals_investment_return <- function(initial_investment,
final_value, fees_paid) {
  total_return <- final_value - fees_paid
  roi <- (total_return / initial_investment) * 100
  return(roi)
}
# Example values
initial_investment <- 5000  # Replace with the initial investment in
Precious Metals
final_value <- 7500  # Replace with the final value of the investment
fees_paid <- 100  # Replace with any fees or transaction costs
# Calculate Precious Metals Investment Return in R
metals_roi <- calculate_metals_investment_return(initial_investment,
final_value, fees_paid)
print(paste("Precious Metals Investment Return (R):", metals_roi, "%"))
```

```python
#Python Example
# Function to calculate Precious Metals Investment Return
def calculate_metals_investment_return(initial_investment, final_value,
fees_paid):
    total_return = final_value - fees_paid
    roi = (total_return / initial_investment) * 100
    return roi
# Example values
initial_investment = 5000   # Replace with the initial investment in
Precious Metals
final_value = 7500  # Replace with the final value of the investment
fees_paid = 100  # Replace with any fees or transaction costs
# Calculate Precious Metals Investment Return in Python
metals_roi = calculate_metals_investment_return(initial_investment,
final_value, fees_paid)
print("Precious Metals Investment Return (Python):", metals_roi, "%")
```

Output
R [1] "Precious Metals Investment Return (R): 148 %"
Python
Precious Metals Investment Return (Python): 148.0 %

References and Links

#R

Chan, N. H. (2011). *Time series: Applications to finance with R and S-Plus* (Vol. 837). John Wiley & Sons. Book Link

Tsay, R. S. (2014). *An introduction to analysis of financial data with R.* John Wiley & Sons. Book Link

Pfaff, B. (2016). *Financial risk modelling and portfolio optimization with R.* John Wiley & Sons. Book Link

Crawley, M. J. (2012). *The R book.* John Wiley & Sons. Book Link

Tsay, R. S. (2013). *Multivariate time series analysis: with R and financial applications.* John Wiley & Sons. Book Link

Arratia, A. (2014). Computational finance. *An Introductory Course with R, Atlantis Studies in Computational Finance and Financial Engineering, 1.* Book Link

Gilli, M., Maringer, D., & Schumann, E. (2019). *Numerical methods and optimization in finance.* Academic Press. Book Link

Danielsson, J. (2011). *Financial risk forecasting: The theory and practice of forecasting market risk with implementation in R and Matlab.* John Wiley & Sons. Book Link

Miranda, M. J., & Fackler, P. L. (2004). *Applied computational economics and finance.* MIT press. Book Link

Lindström, E., Madsen, H., & Nielsen, J. N. (2018). *Statistics for finance.* CRC Press. Book Link

#Python

Hilpisch, Y. (2021). Financial Theory with Python. " O'Reilly Media, Inc.". Book Link

Hilpisch, Y. (2018). *Python for finance: mastering data-driven finance.* O'Reilly Media. Book Link

Lewinson, E. (2020). *Python for Finance Cookbook: Over 50 recipes for applying modern Python libraries to financial data analysis.* Packt Publishing Ltd. Book Link

Kelliher, C. (2022). *Quantitative Finance with Python: A Practical Guide to Investment Management, Trading, and Financial Engineering.* CRC Press. Book Link

Yan, Y. (2017). Python for Finance. Packt Publishing Ltd. Book Link

Humber, M., Humber, M., & Anglin. (2018). *Personal Finance with Python.* Apress. Book Link

Fletcher, S., & Gardner, C. (2010). *Financial modelling in Python.* John Wiley & Sons. Book Link

Garita, M. (2021). *Applied Quantitative Finance.* Springer International Publishing. Book Link

Rogel-Salazar, J. (2018). *Data science and analytics with Python.* CRC Press. Book Link

Johansson, R. (2015). *Numerical Python: A Practical Techniques Approach for Industry.* Apress. Book Link

Yudin, A., & Yudin, A. (2021). Essential financial tasks done with python. *Basic Python for Data Management, Finance, and Marketing: Advance Your Career by Learning the Most Powerful Analytical Tool,* 231-275. Book Link

Korstanje, J. (2021). *Advanced forecasting with Python.* United States: Apress. Book Link

Weiming, J. M. (2015). *Mastering Python for Finance.* Packt Publishing Ltd. Book Link

Alòs, E., & Merino, R. (2022). *Introduction to Financial Derivatives with Python.* CRC Press. Book Link

Aldridge, I., & Avellaneda, M. (2021). *Big data science in finance.* John Wiley & Sons. Book Link

Fratini, S. (2020). Financial Mathematics with Python. Link

Yan, Y. (2014). *Python for finance.* Packt Publishing Ltd. Book Link

Lee, J., Chang, J. R., Kao, L. J., & Lee, C. F. (2023). *Essentials of Excel VBA, Python, and R: Volume II: Financial Derivatives, Risk Management and Machine Learning.* Springer Nature. Book Link

Karasan, A. (2021). *Machine Learning for Financial Risk Management with Python.* " O'Reilly Media, Inc.". Book Link

McKinney, W. (2012). *Python for data analysis: Data wrangling with Pandas, NumPy, and IPython.* " O'Reilly Media, Inc.". Book Link

R & Python Links

https://www.dataquest.io/blog/python-vs-r/
https://posit.co/blog/r-vs-python-what-s-the-best-for-language-for-data-science/
https://posit.co/solutions/
https://www.r-project.org/

Manuals

https://cran.r-project.org/manuals.html

Tutorial

https://ourcodingclub.github.io/tutorials.html

R Studio

https://posit.cloud/content

Online communities for R

https://community.rstudio.com/
https://www.reddit.com/r/Rlanguage/?rdt=45578

https://discuss.ropensci.org/
https://rfordatasci.com/

R packages

https://cran.r-project.org/
https://support.posit.co/hc/en-us/articles/201057987-Quick-list-of-useful-R-packages
https://cran.r-project.org/web/views/
https://cran.r-project.org/web/views/Finance.html
https://cran.r-project.org/web/views/TimeSeries.html
https://bioconductor.org/
https://r-forge.r-project.org/
https://ropensci.org/
https://github.com/
https://kbroman.org/pkg_primer/
https://www.tidyverse.org/

R books for teaching finance

https://www.rmetrics.org

Python programing Links

https://cran.r-project.org/doc/contrib/Paradis-rdebuts_en.pdf
https://www.python.org/about/gettingstarted/

The Python Tutorial

https://docs.python.org/3/tutorial/